D1785664

Web Science: Understanding the Emergence of Macro-Level Features on the World Wide Web

Web Science: Understanding the Emergence of Macro-Level Features on the World Wide Web

Kieron O'Hara

University of Southampton, UK
kmo@ecs.soton.ac.uk

Noshir S. Contractor

Northwestern University, USA
nosh@northwestern.edu

Wendy Hall

University of Southampton, UK
wh@ecs.soton.ac.uk

James A. Hendler

Rensselaer Polytechnic Institute, USA
hendler@cs.rpi.edu

Nigel Shadbolt

University of Southampton, UK
nrs@ecs.soton.ac.uk

the essence of knowledge

Boston – Delft

Foundations and Trends® in Web Science

Published, sold and distributed by:
now Publishers Inc.
PO Box 1024
Hanover, MA 02339
USA
Tel. +1-781-985-4510
www.nowpublishers.com
sales@nowpublishers.com

Outside North America:
now Publishers Inc.
PO Box 179
2600 AD Delft
The Netherlands
Tel. +31-6-51115274

The preferred citation for this publication is K. O'Hara, N. S. Contractor, W. Hall, J. A. Hendler, and N. Shadbolt, Web Science: Understanding the Emergence of Macro-Level Features on the World Wide Web, Foundations and Trends® in Web Science, vol 4, nos 2–3, pp 103–267, 2012

ISBN: 978-1-60198-744-0
© 2013 K. O'Hara, N. S. Contractor, W. Hall, J. A. Hendler, and N. Shadbolt

All rights reserved. No part of this publication may be reproduced, stored in a retrieval system, or transmitted in any form or by any means, mechanical, photocopying, recording or otherwise, without prior written permission of the publishers.

Photocopying. In the USA: This journal is registered at the Copyright Clearance Center, Inc., 222 Rosewood Drive, Danvers, MA 01923. Authorization to photocopy items for internal or personal use, or the internal or personal use of specific clients, is granted by now Publishers Inc. for users registered with the Copyright Clearance Center (CCC). The 'services' for users can be found on the internet at: www.copyright.com

For those organizations that have been granted a photocopy license, a separate system of payment has been arranged. Authorization does not extend to other kinds of copying, such as that for general distribution, for advertising or promotional purposes, for creating new collective works, or for resale. In the rest of the world: Permission to photocopy must be obtained from the copyright owner. Please apply to now Publishers Inc., PO Box 1024, Hanover, MA 02339, USA; Tel. +1-781-871-0245; www.nowpublishers.com; sales@nowpublishers.com

now Publishers Inc. has an exclusive license to publish this material worldwide. Permission to use this content must be obtained from the copyright license holder. Please apply to now Publishers, PO Box 179, 2600 AD Delft, The Netherlands, www.nowpublishers.com; e-mail: sales@nowpublishers.com

Foundations and Trends® in Web Science
Volume 4 Issues 2–3, 2012
Editorial Board

Editor-in-Chief:
Wendy Hall
University of Southampton
wh@ecs.soton.ac.uk
Nigel Shadbolt
University of Southampton
nrs@ecs.soton.ac.uk

Associate Editor:
Kieron O'Hara
University of Southampton
kmo@ecs.soton.ac.uk

Editors

Tim Berners-Lee (MIT)
Noshir Contractor (Northwestern)
Lorrie Cranor (Carnegie Mellon University)
Dieter Fensel (DERI)
Carole Goble (University of Manchester)
Pat Hayes (IHMC)
James Hendler (Rensselaer Polytechnic Institute)
Arun Iyengar (IBM Research)
Craig Knoblock (USC)
Ora Lassila (Nokia Research)
Sun Maosong (Tsinghua University)
Cathy Marshall (Microsoft)
Peter Monge (USC)
Ben Shneiderman (University of Maryland)
Danny Weitzner (MIT)
Yorick Wilks (Oxford Internet Institute)

Editorial Scope

Foundations and Trends® in Web Science will publish survey and tutorial articles in the following topics:

- Agents and the Semantic Web
- Collective Intelligence
- Content Management
- Databases on the Web
- Data Mining
- Democracy and the Web
- Dependability
- Economics of information and the Web
- E-Crime
- E-Government
- Emergent behaviour
- Ethics
- Hypertext/Hypermedia
- Identity
- Languages on the Web
- Memories for Life
- Mobile/Pervasive
- Network Infrastructures
- Performance
- Privacy
- Scalability
- Security
- Semantic Web
- Social Networking
- Standards
- The Law and the Web
- The Web as an Educational Tool
- The Web in the Developing World
- Trust and Provenance
- Universal Usability
- User Interfaces
- Virtual Reality
- Web Art
- Web Governance
- Search
- Web Services

Information for Librarians

Foundations and Trends® in Web Science, 2012, Volume 4, 4 issues. ISSN paper version 1555-077X. ISSN online version 1555-0788. Also available as a combined paper and online subscription.

Foundations and Trends® in
Web Science
Vol. 4, Nos. 2–3 (2012) 103–267
© 2013 K. O'Hara, N. S. Contractor, W. Hall,
J. A. Hendler, and N. Shadbolt
DOI: 10.1561/1800000017

the essence of knowledge

Web Science: Understanding the Emergence of Macro-Level Features on the World Wide Web

Kieron O'Hara[1], Noshir S. Contractor[2], Wendy Hall[3], James A. Hendler[4], and Nigel Shadbolt[5]

[1] *University of Southampton, UK, kmo@ecs.soton.ac.uk*
[2] *Northwestern University, USA, nosh@northwestern.edu*
[3] *University of Southampton, UK, wh@ecs.soton.ac.uk*
[4] *Rensselaer Polytechnic Institute, USA, hendler@cs.rpi.edu*
[5] *University of Southampton, UK, nrs@ecs.soton.ac.uk*

Abstract

In this monograph we consider the development of Web Science since the launch of this journal and its inaugural publication 'A Framework for Web Science' [44]. The theme of emergence is discussed as the characteristic phenomenon of Web-scale applications, where many unrelated micro-level actions and decisions, uninformed by knowledge about the macro-level, still produce noticeable and coherent effects at the scale of the Web. A model of emergence is mapped onto the multitheoretical multilevel (MTML) model of communication networks explained in [252]. Four specific types of theoretical problem are outlined. First, there is the need to explain local action. Second, the global patterns that form when local actions are repeated at scale have to be detected and understood. Third, those patterns feed back into the local, with intricate and often fleeting causal connections to be traced. Finally, as Web Science is an engineering discipline, issues of control of this feedback must be addressed. The idea of a social machine is introduced, where networked interactions at scale can help to achieve goals for people and social groups in civic society; an important aim of Web Science is to understand how such networks can operate, and how they can control the effects they produce on their own environment.

Contents

1

Introduction

The web of our life is of a mingled yarn, good and ill
together.

All's Well That Ends Well, act IV scene iii

This monograph is a distillation of the last seven years' work in
the development of *Web Science*. The idea of the interdisciplinary or
multi-disciplinary science of the Web has been under refinement since
the Web Science Research Initiative (WSRI) was unveiled in late 2006;
a series of theoretical and methodological papers [44, 45, 87, 147, 158,
269, 274, 316, 318, 323] has been published expanding on many themes,
supplemented by an increasing body of work carried out by an increasingly enthusiastic and coherent cohort of researchers and students. The
Web Science Conference has become a growing annual event — 2013
saw the fifth — and is now recognised as an ACM conference. Web
Science courses proliferate at undergraduate and graduate levels, and
attention to the curriculum is growing all the time [87, 370].

We believe that it is timely to revisit the theme of the foundations
of Web Science, already explored at some length in the inaugural article
of this journal [44], but now informed by consideration of some of the

1

significant Web Science research now available. This monograph will explain the motivating issues for Web Science, and show not only how research has addressed the gap between the micro-level processes and the macro-level Web-scale phenomena to which they give rise, but also why research is still needed to do that.

1.1   Scale, Emergence and Control: Social Machines

In particular, we need to place Web Science research in the context of *emergence*, the notion that phenomena visible at larger scales emerge out of interactions that occur at smaller scales, usually at much lower levels of complexity. As explained in the original papers, the otherwise mysterious or under-theorised appearance of macro-level effects can have very large social repercussions (especially given the very large numbers involved — at least 4.45 billion webpages in the indexed Web as of October 2013 (http://www. worldwidewebsize.com/), 2.4 billion people online worldwide as of June 2012 (http://www. internetworldstats.com/stats.htm), a billion active Facebook users [205], 400 million Tweets a day as of March 2013 (http://www.youtube.com/ watch?feature=player embedded&v=Bl-FpuehWGA), 139.7 million blogs on Tumblr as of October 2013 (http://www.tumblr.com/ about), 71 million Wordpress sites as of October 2013 (http://en. wordpress.com/stats/), and 52 billion published and linked Resource Description Framework (RDF) triples in OpenLink Software's Linked Open Data Cloud Cache as of March 2012 (http://www.w3.org/wiki/SweoIG/ TaskForces/CommunityProjects/LinkingOpenData)). For more data on the relationship between the Web and particular nations, see the Web Foundation's Web Index project (http://thewebindex.org/).

It is clear from these very large figures that scale is a major part of the picture for the Web. There are indeed actors, organisations and systems which are very influential, but the scale of the Web precludes straightforward narratives about online developments. The macro-level effects that we see in the online world depend less on the contributions of specified individuals and technologies, than on the convergence of billions of individual decisions to use technologies (often in ways unintended by their designers). Granted the importance of a Mark Zuckerberg or a Jimmy Wales, even such central actors still derive their power from the concerted actions of their billions of users (actions which in turn are also influenced by other structural factors, such as legal constraints, financial and other incentives, network benefits and social norms). The picture is also complicated by the complex relationship between 'online' and 'offline'; it is no longer tenable to assume that there are two different kinds of space, the 'virtual' and the 'real' or 'physical'. Rather, many activities have both online and offline component parts. Finally, the Web is of course evolving and being engineered over time [147], from a web of documents to a web of data, and from a web of people to a network of social networks.

The result, as pointed out by Berners-Lee [41], is a cycle of innovation and reaction that, thanks to the scale, has immense social consequences while lacking policy levers for control. A Web resource is often designed with local interests and assumptions in mind, but the Web itself has many hundreds of millions of users, and billions of pages and connections, so any system can result in emergent phenomena undreamt of by the original designers, whose social assumptions can hardly be expected to be accurate in the general case. Figure 1.1 shows an idea being implemented with some technical work and a set of social

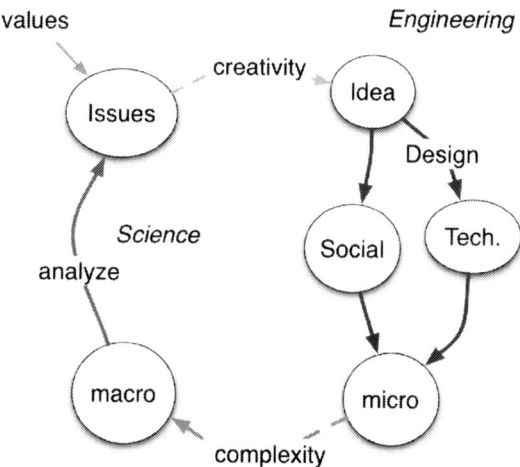

Fig. 1.1 A cycle of engineering and science (from Ref. [41]).

assumptions, to produce a micro-level adjustment to the Web environment, but if enough users take up a system, there will be a marked and noticeable change in macro-level perceptions. It may be that older patterns of behaviour change, or that they are supplemented by new behaviours, or that new users swell the online community (for example, consider the growth of the blogosphere, and how this has changed not only the Web, but also the media, journalism, politics, commerce and social interaction). However that may be, the end result is in effect a new Web understood at the macro-level, as a result of micro-level engineering [269].

This cycle is meant to be illustrative of the difficulties and challenges, rather than a strict ethnographic account of innovation in information technology. In the figure, the micro-level design, when implemented at scale, produces unintended consequences, for which, more often than not, a technical fix is required, and so another idea is born and so we go round the cycle again. The Web Science problem is to marry these episodes of engineering and analysis under a single conceptual framework, and then to achieve a greater level of control of the issues that emerge once the idea is implemented and applied, a marriage which has been referred to as 'philosophical engineering' [314], in which the neat, specifiable world of the realist needs to be reconciled with the scruffier, underdetermined constructed world that defies classification and prediction, and which most of us would perhaps recognise more readily.

Figure 1.2, following David De Roure, gives a sense of different interaction modes of computing. Web Science is concerned with scale — in

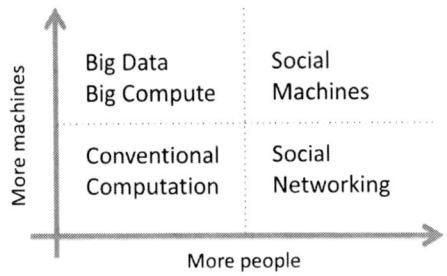

Fig. 1.2 A matrix showing the affordances of scale (adapted from Ref. [99]).

other words, its domain consists of all but the lower left quadrant. Wherever there are more machines, to produce the big data paradigm at upper left, or more people, as in the social networking paradigm at lower right, distribution is inevitable, and hence Web or Web-like technologies will be necessary to handle interaction at scale. The aim of Web Science is not simply to track or monitor the development of such areas, but rather to enhance the technological affordances, and, in time, move technologies upward and toward the right, ultimately to reach the fourth quadrant. We unpack this compressed image later, via Figure 6.1 in Section 6.5.2.

This fourth quadrant is termed as 'social machines' [40, 156], which will be discussed in more detail later in Section 6.5. Yet this concept is implicit in the interpretation of Web Science as a means for understanding the emergence of phenomena at scale, abetted by digital technologies and open networked communications. Computers have always been sociotechnical systems, embedded in organisations, or serving the purposes of users for work or leisure. However, thanks to the spread of interactive read/write technologies (e.g., wikis, photo-sharing, blogging) and devices and sensors embedded in both physical and digital worlds (e.g., GPS-enabled hand-held devices), people and machines have become increasingly integrated. Terms such as 'augmented reality' and 'mediated reality' are in common use [189], and the embedding of computation into society via personal devices has led to the idea of social machines and/or social computation as an abstract conception in which people and machines interact for problem-solving. The 'components' of the machine may be people or computers; the 'routines' or 'procedures' could be carried out by humans, computers or both together.

Social machines are rapidly becoming a focus of computing research [47]. 'Programming the global computer' or 'global ubiquitous computing' has been recognised as a grand challenge for computing [201], while peer-to-peer technologies flexibly link people and computers, as explored in projects such as SOCIAM (http://sociam.org/), OpenKnowledge (http://www.openk.org/) and the Social Computer community (http://www.socialcomputer.eu/). As Web Science begins to unravel the mysteries of scale and control, it will intuitively become the theory and practice of social machines. The aim will be not just to understand the emergent phenomena, but rather to develop means, methods and tools for controlling large-scale phenomena, at least partially. Hence via another route we once more reach the conclusion that analysis and engineering must sit alongside each other within Web Science. The problem is sharpened by the desideratum that 'programming the social computer' must be achievable from *within* the social computer — the methods of Web Science should output policy for governments and large organisations, but will also democratise control by allowing people to develop social machines to achieve their own smaller-scale, local, idiosyncratic purposes.

1.2   A Research Roadmap: Essential Perspectives

In its short history, Web Science has developed a community, and a diverse set of theories and methods, has begun to gather evidence, and is working to enable designers and policymakers to ensure that the Web's effects on society are broadly beneficial, while preserving the invariant general principles that ensure the good health of the Web itself. Scale is important: large linked networks of resources, infrastructure, people and ideas will foster innovation. Secondly, 'good enough' works: bottom-up mechanisms with significant margins for error will foster large user communities. And thirdly, open standards rule [147]. When these principles come together, emergent phenomena can develop at scale.

Dutton [114] has argued that Web Science has a computational bias, inclined to support the efforts of engineers, as opposed to the more social and political orientation of the wider field of Internet Studies. Indeed, this is an important role for Web Science, as 'programming' social machines by designing in desired macro-level effects is conceptually hard to do; a system or tool designer can typically understand and aim for specific micro-level effects, but theories and tools for determining what will emerge at scale out of many such individual actions are sorely lacking [273]. Emergence, explicitly or implicitly, has featured prominently as Web Science has tried to map, connect and theorise the micro and the macro into a coherent account of how social machines emerge when large quantities of computers are deployed by large numbers of networked people. It is unlikely that deterministic theories of social machines will be developed, but it is to be hoped that a greater understanding of the structuring factors and the relative contributions of certain types of structure will result from such analysis.

In order to achieve that, the Web needs to be understood from a variety of perspectives (cf. [44, 45, 158, 314]); no single perspective will encompass the range of relevant phenomena. The research roadmap of Web Science must emphasise at least five relevant perspectives.

- **Computational.** With the emergence of the linked data Web and Semantic Web a key challenge is how to find, browse, explore and query data, rather than documents, at scale (cf. [44], pp. 7–52).
- **Mathematical.** Billions of Web pages are dynamically generated, existing for the period of a particular query or transaction; modelling this transient or ephemeral Web is an urgent requirement (cf. [44], pp. 53–71).
- **Social.** The dynamics and drivers of people's use of newly emergent forms of the Web remain unclear. Yet these will have implications for our understanding of key sociological categories, such as kinship, gender, race, class and community, and vice versa, as they play out online (cf. [44], pp. 73–98).
- **Economic.** Web 2.0/Web 3.0 create many opportunities for users to generate content and share it in self-forming networks, and these need to be modelled in economic terms of incentives and rationality (cf. [354]).
- **Legal/regulatory.** The law, currently reactive to hyperfast Web evolution, should surely lead the intellectual agenda and interact and respond to economic, social and technological influences. The present intellectual property, data protection, torts and policing regulatory regimes, established in the offline world, have to be fit for purpose in the Web 2.0/Web 3.0 environment (cf. [44], pp. 99–109).

These are the kinds of issue studied by the Web scientist, bridging many disciplines. It is worth noting that even if there is a computational/engineering bias in Web Science, social studies (represented by the final three of the five perspectives) are a vital part of the Web scientist's toolbox. As Dutton puts it, Web Science and Internet Studies both "assume that macro-level societal implications can flow from the micro-level decisions made about the Web's protocols" [114, p. 16]. A recent outline of a series of research questions to accompany a social scientist's examination of any Web phenomenon, concerning its relations with analogous offline phenomena, its characteristics, threats, opportunities and effects on other existing activities and relationships [346, p. 69], would not be out of place in a Web Science primer.

1.3   Integrative Research Themes

Another approach to scoping Web Science is to describe the research challenges that aggregate the above perspectives. Although many disciplines quite properly include the study of the Web in their scope, there are certain themes that seem especially characteristic of the Web and its role in communication and practice.

- **Collective intelligence.** Light rules of co-ordination between collaborators can lead to the emergence of large-scale, coherent resources (such as Wikipedia). We need to understand, from a technical point of view, how to enable collective intelligence, as well as to outline the socio-economic reasons for which individuals participate in collective endeavour, the legal frameworks governing the resources created, the policy levers that work in this space and the ethical limits to the use of such policies.
- **Openness.** The Web is a complex mixture of open, public areas and closed, private zones. There are arguments for both: for instance, innovation can be fostered both by information and data sharing, and by protected intellectual property rights. We need to understand which stance is appropriate when. Is openness compatible with the security requirements of e-health applications, for example?

- **Dynamics.** The Web is changing at a rate which may be greater than our ability to observe it; we need to instrument the Web, log it and identify trends.
- **Security, privacy and trust.** All economic, social and legal interactions are based on certain assumptions: that individuals can verify identities, rely on the rules and institutions governing the interactions, and be assured that certain information will remain private. These assumptions are challenged by the Web [50], yet — as recent security revelations concerning the US NSA and the UK GCHQ show (http://www.theguardian.com/world/the-nsa-files, and Ref. [162] for an early academic attempt to place these revelations in perspective) — trust in the infrastructure and in the treatment of one's communications and data will always be an extremely important factor in the growth and development of the Web.
- **Inference and information processing.** The amount of information on the Web is enormous and growing exponentially (it is a major challenge to measure it, never mind to assess how much of it is useful or original). In addition, it comes in a huge range of formats from a vast number of disparate sources. Given this radically decentralised heterogeneity, methods are needed to browse, explore and query the Web in contextually sensitive ways at scale.

It should be clear that each of these themes expresses problems requiring answers from each of the disciplinary perspectives from the research roadmap in Section 1.2. Note also how emergent effects are important factors in these themes. How does collective intelligence emerge from the aggregation of individual contributions? How does openness affect the incentives for innovators, and the take-up (network effects) of their innovations? How do we describe, model and influence the feedback loops between the micro and the macro? How do privacy and trust survive visibility to networks which are much wider, and much more informationally retentive, than social networks which are not digitally mediated? How will the inferences an individual is able to make affect his/her behaviour online — or in other words, how does inference affect micro–macro feedback? In each theme the micro–macro distinction is foregrounded.

1.4 Structure of this Monograph

In this monograph, we review the state of Web Science in 2013–2014 within two research frameworks designed to enable the study of multilevel phenomena. In Section 2, we set out these frameworks, the concept of emergence in the philosophy of science [173], and the Multitheoretical, Multilevel Analytic theory of social networks [252]. Each of these frameworks determines a four-part classification of emergent phenomena, which can be mapped onto each other, and Sections 3–6 will explore these four classes in turn. Section 7 will then bring the four themes back together again in a conclusion.

Sections 3–6 will each be illustrated by a series of exemplary study areas. It goes without saying that Web Science encompasses a wide range of possible objects of study, and so no paper such as this one could possibly be comprehensive. Certain problems, methods or research programmes will be outlined and briefly discussed — these issues have been chosen in order to illustrate certain of the perspectives of the research roadmap above (Section 1.2), or the research themes of Web Science (Section 1.3), as described at the beginning of each of these sections. Before that, however, the rationale for the structure of this monograph will be provided, with some considerations about the overarching theme of emergence.

2

Emergence

What is the city but the people?

Coriolanus, act III scene i

The concept of emergence was explicitly theorised by John Stuart Mill under the term 'heteropathy' [243, 247], and it remains the locus of deep philosophical discussion. Much of that discussion has been driven by puzzles about the mind and specifically consciousness, theorised by some as emerging from physical phenomena in the brain. The recent research programme for a Brain Activity Map is an attempt to understand the determination of neuro-function from the activities of billions of neurons, and is a classic statement of the scientific problems of emergence [11]. Emergence is also a factor in other fields; for instance, the behaviour of an economy based on the individual financial decisions of its members is hard to track, and harder to drive via economic policy [118, 233]. Despite the ubiquity of the idea, there is little sign of consensus emerging about emergence, even concerning its definition [32]. However, for the purposes of this monograph we do not need to be precise about the meaning of the term. If we leave ourselves to think in

11

broad terms, emergence suggests that the phenomena it denotes have a number of characteristics.

1. Emergence contrasts with reduction. If a phenomenon emerges from a lower-level set of phenomena, we can take that to imply that it cannot simply be reduced to a complex proposition about the lower-level phenomena. As an example of reduction, heat is equivalent to the kinetic energy of particles, and a complete description of the particles would tell you all you needed to know about heat — a reductive explanation. On the other hand, arguably, if consciousness is a phenomenon emergent on states of the brain, knowing all there is to know about the brain will still leave us short of an explanation of consciousness.

2. Emergence contrasts with epiphenomenalism. Emergent phenomena are not simply epiphenomena of lower-level phenomena; they have causal powers and laws of their own which go beyond the causal powers of the lower-level phenomena.

3. Emergence is linked to, but not identical with, supervenience. A higher-level phenomenon supervenes on lower-level phenomena when changes at the higher level entail changes at the lower level, but not vice versa. Emergent phenomena therefore supervene on lower levels. However, supervienience does not entail emergence; if X entails Y as a matter of logic, then X supervenes on Y, but does not emerge from Y [188]. A father is a man, but fatherhood does not emerge from manhood.

4. There is an epistemological gap. We cannot simply deduce an emergent phenomenon from a description of the lower-level phenomena from which it emerges.

5. Emergence implies a greater level of complexity. Lower-level phenomena are simpler to describe, but when composed they produce the more complex phenomena which emerge from them.

These considerations assume a division of levels of analysis, where higher-level descriptions supervene on lower-level descriptions. When we consider this supervenience, there are four areas which we need to understand.

1. Local action. What are the interactions and incentives that operate at the local level?
2. Pattern matching. How can we recognise macro-level phenomena? What experiments do we need to do? What instruments do we need?
3. Feedback. What are the links between micro-level and macro-level phenomena (in both directions, as we assume, as the macro-level is emergent, that they both have different causal powers, and so changes at each level can cause changes at the other)?
4. Control. How can we harness the feedback processes to produce beneficial outcomes?

Depending on how the lower levels influence the upper levels, the emergence can either be synchronic or diachronic. In the former type of emergence, the lower level events constitute the higher level emergent events, while in the latter type there is a time lag between the low-level events and the observed emergent higher level phenomena.

The influences on a set of phenomena at a particular level are likely to be of several types [197]:

i. Microdetermination (causal influence from lower levels).
ii. Macrodetermination (causal influence from above).
iii. Structuration (a two-way causal influence).
iv. Externalities (influence from processes outside the total structure).
v. Feedback (influence at a level from within the level).

These five influence types are reasonably intuitive, with the possible exception of the sociological idea of structuration [132, 131], which has a more technical meaning which we will therefore pause to explain in more detail. In a structuration relation, actors are neither totally constrained by the social, economic and political structures within which they operate, nor totally free to ignore these and pursue their own preferences or ideas of the good. Structuration theory maps the complex interplay between the free choices that people make in pursuit of the satisfaction of their preferences, and the structuring principles that limit the range of choices that people will consider. These limits to choice are not necessarily to be perceived negatively — they help reduce the cognitive load for people as they decide how to act. Ultimately, the roots of this kind of theory go back centuries — for instance, in the eighteenth century Edmund Burke's [74] conservative philosophy posited the interplay between liberty and constraint in terms of institutions and tradition.

Structuration is relevant to Web Science because that is what the technology does — it provides a series of constraints on behaviour, while also affording opportunities. Lessig [210] has characterised the constraints on Web users as being created jointly by four separate types of interaction with very different properties and control nexuses: (i) the code written to implement systems; (ii) the economic incentives governing behaviour; (iii) the regulation of the network; and (iv) the social norms governing behaviour. Yet constraints from all these sources also provide opportunity. For instance, a Facebook user can now socialise in previously unanticipated ways, and these new affordances are clearly felt to be valuable by many people (judging by the size of the active Facebook population). However, those affordances are also limiting. Facebook restricts the expressivity of the medium, insisting on particular formats of self-presentation and also basing its funding model on pervasive surveillance. In liberal theory, surveillance of this level is typically argued to be highly detrimental to autonomy [305], but it is hard to argue that the new affordances of social media, including the ability to define and present multiple identities, have diminished freedom. The interplay between constraints and opportunity is the province of structuration theory.

Structuration provides a frame for understanding behaviour that tries to balance the separate influences of structures on the one hand and the agency of the individual on the other. The structures constrain people's choices, but equally, although they are the medium for choice and decision-making by individuals, they are also affected by the decisions people make. Constraining structures have a dynamic driven by use and practice. Structuration has been an important theoretical tool for some years in understanding how people and technology interact [176, 282], and especially as a means of avoiding technological determinism or illegitimately privileging the technical side of a dual relationship [102].

2.1 Emergence on the Web

One simple binary division of levels would be between macro-level phenomena and micro-level phenomena. In the case of the World Wide Web, the micro-level phenomena can be divided into several important subtypes (we do not pretend that this list is exhaustive).

(a) **Individual actors.** The Web is a communication medium which connects individuals with communication needs. These individuals may represent corporations or organisations, or may be acting for their own benefit (various social constraints and economic incentives). They may even be artificial agents. They may be in listening, broadcasting or interacting mode. The communications may concern ideas or resources.

(b) **Protocols, standards, etc.** The Web is described and specified by a series of protocols, formalisms and languages, for example standards set via painstaking processes under the aegis of the World Wide Web Consortium (W3C). Changes in definition, or new definitions, can radically affect actors' online behaviour, as when the invention of Ajax allowed simple asynchronous communication, which in turn helped facilitate the growth of what has been labelled Web 2.0 or the 'social web.'

(c) **Algorithms.** Various automatic processes occur on the web, or using Web resources, which create important affordances. Some are deep in the communications infrastructure, such as the processes (like routing) that keep the Internet efficient. Some are central to the usability of the Web, most obviously the PageRank algorithm that was the basis of Google's search engine.

(d) **Names and naming processes.** The Web depends on social processes of negotiation and curation. Sets of uniform resource identifiers (URIs) need to be curated and managed in order to function well and stably as names for resources accessible via the Web. Certain interest groups will devote energy to the development and curation of reference ontologies of key terms.

(e) **Web pages and other resources.** The Web itself is made up of billions of pages (the so-called *shallow Web*), and many other data resources (the *deep Web*), linked together. The Web is always evolving as pages, data and links appear and disappear, and is therefore a dynamic structure.

(f) **Web-based spaces, organisations or networks.** Certain groups — e.g., Google, Facebook, Amazon, eBay, Baidu, Alibaba, Twitter, Wikileaks, Wikipedia, Anonymous, World of WarCraft, Second Life — provide a platform for transformational events which can influence online and offline life. They gain offline influence by the large-scale networks they are able to host online.

(g) **Companies and other organisations.** There is sometimes a relationship between a website (e.g., the Google search engine or the gmail system) and a company (e.g., Google) which runs it. On the basis of the large takeup of online services, some companies can come to be extremely large, influential and valuable.

(h) **Nations and supranational organisations (such as the EU).** These often have an interest in promoting a particular view of what the Web should facilitate, and often either have or wish to obtain influence over such organisations as ICANN or the W3C, as well as providing the business environment in which businesses and websites operate. eBay's business model of a mediated commercial transaction space was damaged when the French government prevented a sale of Nazi memorabilia, while Google's search engine suffered interference from the Chinese government. Nations also affect the Web by promoting such factors as broadband, English language (or other language) education, the spread of laptops or mobile devices, anti-money laundering regulations, surveillance schemes, anti-spamming rules, etc.

(i) **Organisations that control the infrastructure upon which the Web relies.** This infrastructure includes the Internet, the telecommunications infrastructure, the electricity supply and the devices developed to access the Web.

The Web can be 'defined' or understood in terms of its agents, its protocols, its processes or its topological structure alone, but it is clear that such accounts will not be complete or comprehensive. Any analyses or predictions that they entail will only cover a small fraction of the relevant variables. The macro-level phenomena that emerge from the Web depend on the complex interplay of all these components.

How does emergence manifest itself as an issue for the Web? If we consider the zone of time in which an action may make a difference, what Schön [311, p. 62] has called the *action-present*, which depends on the pace of activity and the boundaries of potential action, we find it is both tiny and vast, depending on point of view. The cycles of Web development are measured in years. Blogging took a number of years to develop from small beginnings, and then 'suddenly' took off at the beginning of the century. 'Suddenly' in this case is still a matter of years from, say, the appearance of the first blogging tools and guides and the first major political issues influenced by bloggers in 2001 and 2002, to the exponential growth characteristic of the years after 2004. But what counts is the timescale of an effective intervention. The phenomenal growth of the blogosphere was predicted by very few, and its specific effects on political discourse or the offline media were anticipated by even fewer. The timescale is certainly large enough for technical development, but the social context evolves alongside the technical as well as driving it. What seems imperative in year 0 of a research project may be completely out of date by year 3 when a product appears [118, 273].

New types of online behaviour become very popular very quickly. At the time of writing (2013), Facebook and Twitter dominate thinking about cutting-edge large-scale Web phenomena, but by, say, 2018 it is quite possible that the landscape will be very different and the giants of five years previously will be hopelessly out of date (consider how quickly the once-mighty MySpace declined). Datasets for large-scale modelling are extremely important to alleviate this issue (cf. Section 4.5). Such analyses are clearly ways forward, but as each new star application comes along, new actors (possibly responding to different incentives) may arrive with it, rendering old assumptions void. Not only that, but a five or six year development and growth cycle will take many of the most enthusiastic users from adolescence to adulthood with all the attitudinal changes that implies. In short, the scale of the phenomena means that what seems a relatively long action-present for Web Science is in reality very curtailed. By the time data are gathered, models created and simulations run, the opportunity to influence events may already be past. Getting the data right is a vital part of understanding emergent phenomena [173, pp. 79–80]. As an analogy, entomologists' understanding of ant colonies took off once it was understood that colonies behaved differently depending how old they were. Until data from several years was available to give a diachronic account, colonies tended to be studied over a period of weeks, and therefore it remained unappreciated that the lifespan of a colony was equivalent to the life of its queen, which could be up to 15 years. Younger colonies behave differently to older ones in ways which were invisible to scientists until the right kind of data were gathered [139]. This is the type of data gathering and study that we need to do for the Web (see Section 4.5).

Actions that affect the Web are carried out at the micro-level. Such micro-level actions, performed by agents of the nine respective types above, might include:

(a) **Individual actors.** A person posts a photograph on Flickr.

(b) **Protocols and standards.** The W3C develops a standard for a formalism to express, say, trust in the Semantic Web.

(c) **Algorithms.** Someone develops, implements or installs a spam detection system.

(d) **Names.** The owners of a network reorganise the local URIs.

(e) **Web pages.** The author of a webpage adds links to, or removes them from, his/her page.

(f) **Web-based spaces.** A social networking site changes its privacy policy.

(g) **Companies.** A company monetises the data it holds about its users, selling the data to market research organisations.

(h) **Nations.** A nation or supranational organisation sponsors scientific research in a particular area to promote particular Web solutions or institutions.

(i) **Infrastructure organisations.** A telecommunications company makes a business decision about the implementation or otherwise of a mobile network.

Each one of these actions will alter the Web directly or indirectly in a tiny way. Typically they will not have a noticeable effect beyond the local. Each of the actions would be performed because of local considerations, needs or incentives. None of them will necessarily have been performed for the public good.

And yet they could all be part of major social movements detectable at the macro-level on the Web. They all affect the Web in combination with many millions of related actions. This is reminiscent of Warren Weaver's discussion of the ascent from simple systems with a small number of variables, to disorganised complexity characterised by millions of variables, to what he called *organised complexity* [371]. The lower-level systems listed above (agents, variables) are examples of disorganised complexity, characterised by a high number of variables and their amenability to statistical analysis. But when we consider these systems composed and integrated, an order emerges which, in Weaver's words, "involve[s] dealing simultaneously with a sizeable number of factors which are interrelated into an organic whole."

2.2 Theories of Emergence and Structure

This is a common situation. Interestingly, it has been argued that even apparently formal structures (such as firms and organisations) are best studied as emergent structures, because much of the power of such formal organisations lies in what emerges from informal networks of interaction [187, 200]. The networks in which someone participates are not homogeneous, however, and there may be very complex interactions between them [301], and even interference between overlapping networks that reduces their joint effectiveness [252, p. 10].

The binary division between disorganised and organised complexity is a simplification that powerfully motivates the theoretical and engineering challenge, while somewhat misrepresenting the reality. Many phenomena go beyond the actions of individuals — for instance, Facebook is influential partly because it is a single entity with over a billion members (larger than all but the most populous states in the world), but of course the actions of those people also make Facebook what it is (actions mediated by the structures that Facebook has created). Clearly the story of how the Web works cannot be a simple one, and must account for how it constrains its users and simultaneously supports very creative uses.

Hence we should be wary of any simple account of how an individual's behaviour is influenced, or of the ideological belief that the code with which the Web is written will license the most decent behaviour. As Mancur Olson suggested many years ago, the visibility of anti-collective or free riding behaviour (such as spamming) will, via social norms (and regulation), have a powerful effect on whether such behaviour is carried out [280], and the Web thus far is a space which is peculiarly conducive to invisibility. The social norms that could bind anti-social behaviour cannot necessarily operate in the dark of the Web (which is not to say that the dark Web does not contain recognisable analogues to 'ordinary' Web phenomena such as eBay — see Section 4.4). Similarly, while government and corporate surveillance are notoriously made easier by digital interactions, the volume of data, the difficulty of determining meaningful patterns of behaviour from noisy data, the fluidity of identity and the (admittedly meagre) protections of privacy and data protection laws mean that the influence of regulations is outweighed by that of the economic incentives [50]. The code, of course, licenses a great deal of anti-social behaviour, which was one of the original motivations for developing Web Science [44, 45].

One way of thinking about the various levels is of the Web as a communication network — "data, information, knowledge, images, symbols, and any other symbolic forms that can move from one point in a network to another or can be cocreated by network members" [252, p. 3] — which is a type of pattern of information that has already been studied from an inclusive perspective to integrate the wide range of theoretical mechanisms that have been proposed to explain the creation, maintenance and dissolution of such patterns [252, pp. 45–70]. The Web is both a communications network, and an opportunity space for communications networks to form.

Monge and Contractor, following an exhaustive survey of the literature into network research [251], argued that the multi-layered set of phenomena that make up any network, the Web included, requires a wider framework than a single level of analysis and a single theoretical account for communication behaviour. They developed their *Multitheoretical, Multilevel Analytic Framework* (MTML — [252]) to bridge the various levels in order to explain both lower-level and emergent behaviour of networks.

2.3 Sampling the Web Science Space Across the MTML Framework

The stages of emergence — local action, patterns, feedback and control — listed in Section 2 above map onto the MTML framework. Although the latter is described primarily in terms of understanding and testing hypotheses about organisational networks, the mapping gives a sense of the levels of analysis and types of theory appropriate for understanding the emergence of macro-level Web phenomena from micro-level actions.

Monge and Contractor [252, p. 56] summarises ten types of predictor variables for the study of communication networks. The major distinction is between endogenous and exogenous variables. *Endogenous* variables are "relational properties inherent in the focal network that influence the realization of that network," and are "characteristics of the relations within the network that are themselves used to explain the structural tendencies of that relation" [252, p. 55]. Endogenous variables can be expressed at one of four levels: a single individual, dyadic relations between two individuals, triadic relations between three individuals, and the global level of the whole network.

The first three types of endogenous variables, individual, dyadic and triadic, all relate to the Web Science issue of how local action emerges, and what are its properties. What influences it, and how does it affect the network? Issues that the network analysis are concerned with include centrality and autonomy (individual level), mutuality and reciprocation (dyadic level), and transitivity and cyclicality (triadic level). For Web Science, these constructs, and the types of theory which help explain these sorts of pattern (theories such as social capital theory [77], exchange theory [93] and balance theory [155]), help pose and answer questions to do with why individuals behave as they do online, why they make the decisions they do, what drives them to or away from particular websites, or the Web as a whole.

So, an example Web Science issue for the endogenous local would be how to maintain trust between the members of a network. What signals would have to be sent and consumed, and what institutional relationships would need to be in place in order for warranted trust to flourish? Explanations of local action, focusing on endogenous local variables, will be discussed in Section 3.

As noted, a monograph of this size must be selective about which research areas it covers. In Section 3, we will focus on issues relating to the networks and relationships of individuals who interact (or not) with the Web. We will report on and review research on why and when individuals engage with social networks online (Section 3.1), why and when they trust others (Section 3.2), and whether or not the technology is affecting offline networks, leading to alienation (Sections 3.3 and 3.4).

The fourth type of endogenous variable, the endogenous global, corresponds to the Web Science area of pattern matching. What are the properties of the global Web, and how do we spot them? What is the macro-level? Monge and Contractor draw attention to measures such as network density and centralisation in network analysis, and also relevant here are several further efforts to investigate Web topology and other types of measure. Web Science questions here would be about the large-scale patterns on the Web and what could be deduced from them — for example, are there any signatures or patterns characteristic of the dark Web of cybercrime, cyberwarfare and cyberespionage? Are there any patterns which indicate vulnerabilities? These areas will be discussed in Section 4.

This section will look at structures detectable on the Web, conceived both mathematically and socially. Network theory and topography will be discussed in Sections 4.1 and 4.2, particularly focusing on influential work on the Web as a scale-free network. Section 4.3 will take a parallel structural view from the perspective of social science, looking at theories of the information society. Section 4.4 looks at a portion of the Web with special social significance — the so-called 'dark Web' where criminal, subversive or sometimes just clandestine activity takes place. Finally, Section 4.5 discusses an architecture for gathering data in order to find structures and other large-scale phenomena online.

Exogenous variables "refer to variable properties outside the focal network that influence the probability of ties being present or absent in the focal network, that is, its realization", and are "characteristics of the network . . . that are used to explain the structural tendencies." They include "the attributes of the people or other nodes in the network, other relations within the network, as well as the same relation in the network in the previous points in time" [252, p. 55].

Exogenous variables come in two types, which again correspond to aspects of emergence in Web Science. Exogenous actor variables (at the individual, dyadic, triadic and global levels) allow us to explore feedback. The issues here concern the ways in which global properties of the Web have a downwards causal effect influencing individual or global actions. How can we understand the Web as a homeostatic system? An example Web Science issue here would be, for instance, understanding how network structures in Twitter can help predict the probability of particular people being influenced by particular messages. Feedback will be discussed in more detail in Section 5, focusing on issues to do with content provision and influence through online networks, looking at how network structures help explain individuals' behaviour via the network influences upon them.

Exogenous network variables — i.e., relations with other networks and the same network at other periods of time — correspond to the final Web Science issue of control, and how the network itself can be driven in a particular direction, whether intentionally or contingently. So, for example, an issue here is how privacy, which is not a property of the Web as such but rather of the expectations people have of the treatment of their information on the Web, based on norms in a society that exists outside the Web, can be facilitated by systems within the

Web itself, without simultaneously undermining privacy by creating stores of information to which the authorities will demand access or, or simultaneously undermining the Web by slowing down the flow of information [162, 265]. Control issues will be discussed in Section 6.

Section 6.1 will discuss the nature of the control problem in more detail, using the example of the topological patterns already described in Sections 4.1 and 4.2 to provide interesting pointers to the global properties of the Web (Section 6.1.1), and arguing that the Web is the type of large-scale engineered artefact that demands a reflective attitude toward design (Section 6.1.2). The remaining subsections go on to detail some specific engineering efforts to amend or update the Web, or to adapt the Web to particular social functions. Section 6.2 looks at attempts to move from the 'traditional' Web of linked documents to a Web of linked data, including efforts to populate such a Web with open data freely available under unrestrictive licences. Section 6.3 moves on to consider how Web technology has created new political spaces, which themselves affect how the Web develops; we consider recent ideas about Digital Era Governance, the use of linked data and open data technologies to release government data, and the ongoing and politically controversial attempts to engineer privacy. Section 6.4 then looks at ways in which the Web can facilitate personal data management.

Finally, Section 6.5 considers how such developments could lead to the development of social machines, as described above in Section 1.1, allowing the linking of people and devices at scale in such a way as to allow bottom up control of the Web and its affordances, rather than the top down engineering of Web environments by government and the private sector which often determines an individual's online activities. The development of social machines has been an underlying goal of Web engineering since the early days [40].

Figure 2.1 shows the rationale behind this particular sampling of Web Science issues. If we imagine the Web as being co-constituted by individuals and social institutions, then we have chosen our examples to exemplify each causal connection. The influence of individuals on the Web, falling under the headings of local action and control, is highlighted by the adoption of social networking (Section 3.1), the requirements of personal data management (Section 6.4) and the gradual

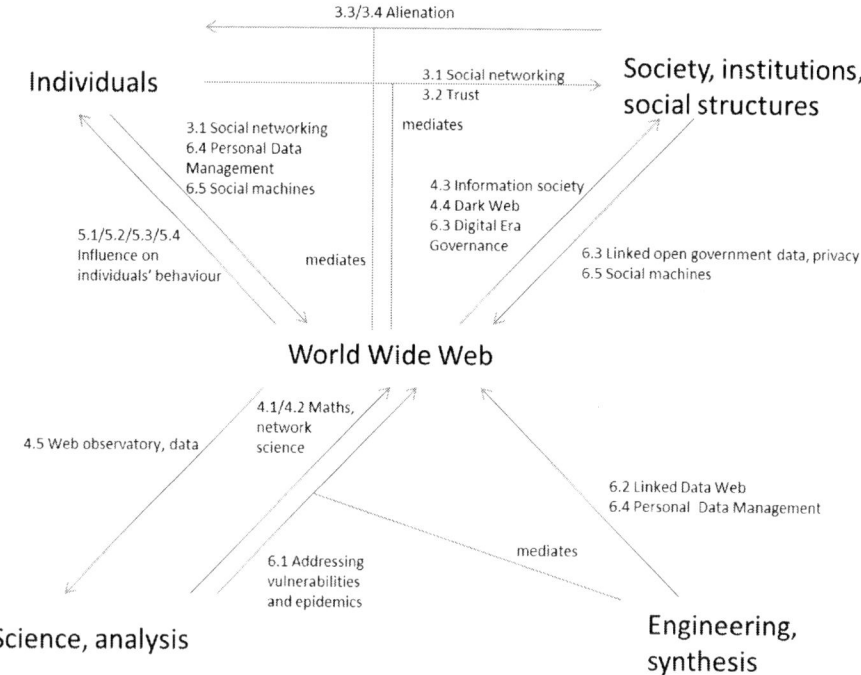

Fig. 2.1 The sample of Web Science issue discussed in this monograph.

appearance of social machines (Section 6.5). The reverse influence of the Web on individuals is a matter of feedback, and is exemplified by the discussion of influence (Section 5). The Web's influence on society is highlighted by some of the patterns we detect, such as the sociological concept of the information society (Section 4.3) and the dark Web (Section 4.4), as well as the idea of Digital Era Governance (Section 6.3). Conversely, there are instances of social control of the Web's development discussed in Section 6, including linked open government data (Section 6.3) and privacy and security (Section 6.3), as well as the creation of social machines (Section 6.5). Furthermore, we also discuss instances where the Web mediates individuals influencing and being influenced by society and its institutions, such as social networking (Section 3.1), trust (Section 3.2), where the direction is from the individual to society, and the issues surrounding alienation (Sections 3.3 and 3.4) where the direction is reversed.

The Web also affects and is affected by intellectual activities such as science and engineering, and those connections are reflected in the lower half of Figure 2.1. Analysis of the Web can tell us about many of its properties, including its topology (Sections 4.1 and 4.2); analysis can change the Web directly, mediated by engineering techniques, when we look at using structure for control, exemplified in this monograph by vulnerabilities and epidemics (Section 6.1). As the Web is a constructed space, engineers often affect it directly; their influence is discussed in detail in areas such as the Linked Data Web (Section 6.2) and personal data management (Section 6.4). Meanwhile, as we instrument the Web, it provides data for analysis and the discovery of patterns (Section 4.5).

The exemplars chosen are meant to be indicative of the spread of influences both to and from the Web, and as argued earlier can hardly be exhaustive, although with our sample we have tried to cover most of the significant directions of influence in the above diagram. They are intended to show the importance of mathematics and science (e.g., Sections 4.2, 6.1), qualitative social science (e.g., Sections 3.3, 4.3, 5.3.2), quantitative social science (e.g., Sections 3.4, 4.4, 5.2, 5.3.1) and engineering (e.g., Sections 6.2, 6.3, 6.4). Ultimately, the hope is that the contributions of all these various types of discipline will empower individuals and social groups to use the Web to achieve their own social goals and pursue their own ideas of the good (Section 6.5).

3

Local Action: The Endogenous Local

I am myself alone.

Henry VI Part III, act V scene vi

The first issue with understanding emergent phenomena is to understand what the local or micro-level actions, structures, institutions, motivations and constraints are. In this section, we consider the action of endogenous variables at the local level, describing the actors on the Web (nodes on the network), or their very local relations. How do actors relate to others; how do pairs, triples or other small numbers interact?

The Web is a social phenomenon — people interact, and largely enjoy interacting, on it. Some have no purpose; others have business reasons; still others have communication or governmental needs. These small-scale interactions are important for creating the macro-scale phenomena that make the Web exciting for some and worrying for others. Yet can we discern anything from the properties of the micro-scale interactions that will tell us about the macro? It is possible to traverse the Web remarkably quickly [9], and so it is often said that the Web, and similar such networks are *small worlds*. Short chains of connection

27

are pervasive, and people are able to find them despite having only knowledge of the very local areas of their networks.

It is not trivial to create this small-world effect if you are a local node in the network without a global picture. If one imagines a geographically-located network (i.e., each node is somewhere in space) such that nodes are connected with their spatial neighbours, and then randomly links some non-adjacent nodes together, one gets a reasonable model of the world; one knows one's neighbours, and some other people, colleagues, dispersed family members, old friends, etc. But such a random network is not a small world — it cannot in general be traversed in a small number of steps.

Such a network becomes a small world is when there is a probability distribution describing when two nodes are linked, where the probability grows as the distance between nodes decreases [369]. If we express this probability as the reciprocal of the distance between the two nodes to some power $\alpha(d(u,v)^{-\alpha})$, then there is a sweet spot where a small world emerges from a network whose nodes only have local knowledge, when $\alpha = 2$ [193]. At this inverse-square distribution, there is a decentralised algorithm for delivering a message which achieves a very rapid delivery time, bounded by a function proportional to the square of the log of the size of the network. Furthermore, $\alpha = 2$ is the only exponent for which such an algorithm can achieve a similarly bounded delivery time. We will discuss the mathematics of this in more detail in Sections 4.1 and 4.2.

The distance metric is fundamental here, and for relatively large and dense networks it proves to be useful to define distance ordinally; the definition is very simple, in that the probability that two nodes m and n connect is proportional to the reciprocal of the number of nodes between them, in the sense of being closer to m than n is [218]. The intuition behind this is that in a 2-D space, as the distance between two nodes increases, the number of nodes between them in the ordinal ranking will increase as to the area of the circle swept out by one node around the other as centre, i.e., as the square of the spatial distance between them (= the radius of the circle). Hence the inverse-square distribution of the previous paragraph becomes linear in the ordinal rank. Using such ordinal metrics, it has been possible to confirm Kleinberg's theoretical result with real-world online social networks, including Live-Journal [218] and Facebook [24].

3.1 Engaging with a Social Network Online

Online social networking has been an important growth area on the Web since the beginning of Web Science in 2006 (for instance, although they were mentioned, online social networks were not prominent in the issues covered in a previous survey for this journal — [44]). We should begin here by drawing a distinction between a social network — a social phenomenon that is independent of the Web or the Internet and already the subject of many decades of sociological research [140] — and a *social networking site* (SNS), which is a website that is intended to facilitate social networking. In this monograph, the term 'social network' will refer to a set of relationships between human beings, while we will reserve the term 'SNS' for entities such as MySpace, Friendster and Facebook. The people with whom one networks on an SNS may be friends, acquaintances or colleagues in an offline context, or the site may provide the only connection. The site will no doubt reflect many facets of the relationships one has, but can only be partially reflective of the social network conceived as a whole. Of course, being digital, the site will furnish researchers, advertisers and other snoopers with vast quantities of data, dwarfing the data about the network to be gained from other sources, but we need to be alert to the fact that the picture will be extremely partial even when it is not misleading.

SNSs have developed rapidly since they first attracted academic attention. After a mere six years, boyd and Ellison felt the need to revise an earlier definition of an SNS given in a survey paper [67] after the technical affordances of such sites evolved rapidly, for instance as media streaming became more prominent and as profiles became more dynamic and collaborative. The definition minted in 2013 reads:

> A social network site is a *networked communication platform* in which participants 1) have *uniquely identifiable profiles* that consist of user-supplied content, content provided by other users, and/or system-level

> data; 2) can *publicly articulate connections* that can be
> viewed and traversed by others; and 3) can consume,
> produce and/or interact with *streams of user-generated
> content* provided by their connections on the site [118,
> p. 158].

This definition reflects the fact that profiles have moved on from being
fairly static and fixed self-presentational messages to being expressions
of intention and attitude, nodes related to various different groups, and
repositories of data (only some of which is supplied by the owner of the
profile). SNS architectures now encourage the profile to be affected or
adjusted by activities and streams of data, so that the profile has a
life of its own. Connections (friendships) have become valuable com-
modities, sets of relations across networks — the *social graph* — which
has economic and surveillance potential. Some of that potential rubs
off onto others on the friends list; the fact that X has a set of interests
and X has friended Y could be used to imply that Y is likelier than
usual to have the same set of interests. Friendship lists have become
economically important, and companies now wish to share them (with
potential privacy issues — [263]).

The economic importance of data about interactions, links and
connections between people stems from the possibility of developing
empiricially informed theories about when and how people change opinions or behaviour in certain ways. For instance, data from real-world
but online Web communities has been graphed to illustrate patterns of
influence between friends or associates — when does the behaviour of
your friends influence your behaviour, and how many friends are needed
to tip you into changing behaviour? Analyses of a number of communities and behaviour types, including joining a LiveJournal group [23],
editing a Wikipedia article [95] and publishing at conferences [23], show
similar patterns emerging, where friends influence behaviour. Influence
by a second or a third friend has a greater effect than the first, but
eventually the curve shows diminishing returns. Dong et al. [109] found
that the co-evolution of behaviour and social relationships could be
explained by the rate at which people co-locate at different events. A
'critical mass' effect, whereby a person is sceptical for a while, but

when a sufficient number of his friends behave in a certain way, he is persuaded, does not seem very common.

So, for example, in an interesting study, Bond et al. [55] described an experiment in which positive messages about voting were placed on Facebook during the 2010 mid-term elections in the United States, together with an 'I voted' button to click. The positive messages on their own had no effect above a control group which received no messages. However, there was a 2.2% increase in voting among people who received the messages in addition to the profile pictures of half a dozen Facebook friends who had clicked 'I voted'. This was made up of a 0.4% direct effect from the experimental message, supplemented by a 1.8% increase from the indirect effects of seeing messages (for example in news feeds) about friends' voting. These small but significant increases would appear as noise in a smaller experiment, but the large sample size — 61 million — enabled identification. The consequence of this is that when we look at political interventions, the individual recipient is now not the basic unit of analysis; when an individual is given information about the political process, or about how others in his or her network have behaved, 80% of the total effect found by Bond et al. [55] was not on the individual, but on his or her friends. In political terms, interventions no longer can be evaluated in terms of the effect on the recipient of the intervention, but rather on the effect on the network. This seems to be true even if relatively modest numbers of people use technology to follow elections [299, 300, 324, 325]. The 2012 Presidential campaign by Barack Obama exploited this insight with verve [272].

People seem to choose their online friends based on a certain similarity (or similarity brings people together online), but friends continue to grow more similar for a period after getting an online link — whether this is caused by people changing to be like their friends or the growing network of friends containing more similarity [224]. Similarity appears to be both a cause and an effect of selection. People often get together and become aware of each other's presence via some recent, shared activity around an artefact (such as editing a Wikipedia page), and so the two-way relation between similarity and selection seems not unlikely in that context [95]. This does seem to echo offline relationships — it has been claimed, for example, that obesity, happiness and smoking are all contagious within a network of friends [2, 20, 91, 127]. The data required to perform these experiments is taken from location-sensitive devices which implies an online component to the interactions. Some are sceptical about the value of these analyses [224], but equally there are many strong connections between online and offline social behaviour. Aharony et al. [2] showed a strong correlation between the number of mobile apps people have in common and the amount of face-to-face time they get together.

These are not the only factors that affect whether someone will join a group at a particular stage. Backstrom et al. [23] investigated whether someone's propensity to join a group could be estimated by examining their position in the network, but also looked at the local connections of that person's friends. Their examination of LiveJournal data showed that someone was more likely to join a group which contained a number of their friends if those friends were connected than if the friends were independent of each other.

Group-joining is not in itself necessarily a good thing. In the offline world, independent contacts and contacts outside a tightly knit local friendship group are more effective means of promoting economic development [77], and we see similar phenomena from online data. Eagle et al. [115] have shown, in a study based on telephone and mobile phone data, that the diversity of a population's contacts (i.e., the proportion of contacts that are not linked to each other) is positively correlated with economic well-being. Aharony et al. [2] have shown from very rich data from real-world situations gathered with the consent of the subjects that as individuals' income falls, so does their social diversity. The network does not tend to survive the fall in income.

3.2 Trust

Data from the Web can help us infer theories about trust. Social networks provide a platform for creating connections that usually go under the name of 'friendship' — such a connection has a positive connotation. However, trust can be counterbalanced by lack of trust (lack of a connection), mistrust and distrust (a negative judgment on a contact), and data can be supplied on these matters too. It is possible to infer varying qualities of relationships even in an SNS such as Facebook (cf. [118, pp. 155–157]); for instance, one study examined the effect of Facebook on social capital depending on types of activity (contrasting one-on-one communication, broadcasts to wider audiences, and passive consumption of social news), and individual differences among users, including social communication skill and self-esteem. Receiving messages from friends was associated with increases in social capital, but other messages were not [76].

Some sites explicitly tag connections with positive or negative connotation. Epinions (http://www.epinions.com/), a consumer review site begun in 1999, allows its users to rate reviews as 'very helpful', 'helpful', 'somewhat helpful', 'not helpful' and 'off topic', while members can 'trust' or 'block' each other. The order in which reviews appear for a member depends on the ratings of that member's reviews and his/her own ratings of other members. The technology news website Slashdot (http://slashdot.org/) has a peer-driven content management system with which articles and comments are rated, and fellow users can be selected as 'friend' or 'foe'. On other sites, certain actions can be aggregated and used to infer trust and mistrust. For instance, on Wikipedia, editors are promoted within the administrative structure on the basis of an open vote [75], while some multi-player online games also involve decisions to trust fellow players or not [3, 339, 340].

Looking at trust between people algorithmically, using network properties of the relationships between people to infer information about levels of trust, is an active area of Web Science research. Golbeck [135] created a website called FilmTrust for film recommendations in which participants rated their trust in other people within the social network. She then demonstrated that algorithms based on the network structure could accurately predict the trust values, and that film recommendations based on people knowing the recommenders were more highly trusted. Similar results have since been replicated for many other areas and in larger scale networks. A review of this literature, and a more general overview of trust on the Web, appears in an earlier volume in this Foundations and Trends series [136], and see also Ref. [44, pp. 90–94] for an earlier Web Science review.

3.3   Alienation

For many individuals, life online may be a tempting way of spending their time, but ultimately may prove unsatisfying, unstimulating or even alienating [79, 202]. In one prominent recent analysis, sociologist and psychologist Sherry Turkle [352] examines our relations with technological artefacts and with other technologically mediated relationships, and finds the future bleak. The burden of her argument is that many of the intricate and intimate nuances of human relationships are being lost as crude technologies are incorporated into our emotional and social lives.

In Turkle's view, technologies start off being 'good enough' to support a particular type of human emotion or relationship. So, for example, the care of elderly people can be provided by appealing and efficient robots. They have the advantages of being always available to help (unlike friends or relatives), having infinite time (unlike hard-pressed nurses), and immune to feelings of guilt. And since they are admittedly incapable of caring, the fact that they don't 'really' care about the elderly person in their care is not as humiliating and dispiriting as a lack of interest on the part of a human nurse or relative would be. So the caring robot is good enough.

She identifies a similar, if less dramatic, process with respect to virtual relations in a digital world, whether mediated through a PC, a mobile phone or other type of portable computational device. Facebook created the 'friend' function, with the end result that our ideas about the complex phenomenon of friendship are being coarsened. One can 'friend' someone quite casually, and 'unfriend' them just as easily. It has long been a concern in many narratives that our Facebook friends are equivalents in our online social network. One can just as easily friend one's next door neighbour as Barack Obama or Sarah Palin (e.g., [126]). Yet our relationships with real-world friends are highly heterogeneous. One shares different confidences, and does different things, with different friends. Friendship inspires loyalty, but to different degrees with different friends and in different spheres of life. Friendship's borderline with love on the one hand, and acquaintance on the other, are very blurred (although it has been argued that people are quite able to discriminate between 'genuine' friendship and SNSs' friendship, for example, being able to answer questions about whether their social network friends are 'actual' friends — [120]).

For Turkle [352, p. 4], the friend function is evidence that we live in a culture of simulation, where authenticity is a problem and a challenge, rather as sex in Victorian England. A holiday or gap year is spent ignoring our exotic surroundings and texting and chatting with friends at home (who may of course also be elsewhere than home — [352, p. 156]). There is certainly a point to be made here, perhaps following Sontag's [329, p. 9] point that, in an age of photography, "travel has become a strategy for accumulating photographs".

Hence, Turkle describes a situation in which people whose relationships are substantially mediated by technology will adapt, simplifying and coarsening their relationships to fit the demands from their permanently-present always-on network (cf. [202]). "[T]he culture in which [the selves formed in online spaces] develop tempts them into narcissistic ways of relating to the world" [352, p. 179], in other words "getting on with others by dealing only with their made-to-measure representations" [352, p. 177]. Similarly, the wired modern crafts his or her appearance to a particular specification. The technology allows even the most trivial communication to be edited and tailored, so that an immediate and the potentially over-revealing instant reaction (such as occurs in face to face interaction or on a telephone) is eliminated [352, p. 187]. We can create ourselves in such a way as to ease our anxieties, but only temporarily. One tries to design one's profile so that it reveals the 'real me', but this merely shifts the agony of interaction with others: who is the 'real me'?

> When a man who, in his real life social contacts, is quiet and bashful, adopts an angry, aggressive persona in virtual reality, one can say that he thereby expresses the repressed side of himself, a publicly non-acknowledged aspect of his 'true personality' — that his 'electronic id is here given wing'; however, one can also claim that he is a weak subject fantasizing about more aggressive behaviour in order to avoid confronting his real

life weakness and cowardice. ([388, pp. 137–138] and cf. [352, pp. 179–186])

As a final step, those who are very digitally immersed — Turkle comments on her interview with Gordon Bell, who has manufactured a massive digital archive of his life [34] — have a tendency to treat anything which is not in the database as something that is either trivial, or effectively non-existent [352, pp. 300–302].

There is an argument to be had about whether this is an inauthentic life, but it connects with a view of the Web (and the Internet) as a space which can lead to tight feedback loops and so-called 'echo chambers' [336, 286]. If people are driven to seek out like-minded people, then in the online world, where distance is reduced, search is easy and one can filter out opposing voices, we may tend to adapt our relationships to the technology that facilitates them by searching for friends and filtering out foes. On this combination of views, the Web could really make things worse, by promoting dangerous feedback loops of radicalism and group polarisation. The Internet, says Turkle, "is more than old wine in new bottles" [352, p. 156].

3.4   Alienation and Context: The Networked Individual

On the other hand, technology is not a homogeneous influence on an individual, and an individual's social context is usually more multi-dimensional. Sociologist Barry Wellman has studied the network connections between individuals (mainly in the US), and argues that the evidence shows that the above scenario is only a partial picture, and does not do justice to the full picture of our complex engagements. We have more friends than ever, we still are importantly anchored in our local environments and our online friends tend to be our offline friends as well, so that the attenuated transactions between online individuals via sculpted avatars that worry commentators play a relatively small role in our lives. Indeed, the division between our online and our offline lives is no longer easy to draw [368, 376], and also see the multitude of reports from the Pew Internet and American Life project, http://pewinternet.org/).

Wellman argues that the growth of the Web, and social network sites in particular, has provided an opportunity for people to leave tight-knit and constricting groups, and to live in looser networks. People have generally moved from being group members to being individuals, albeit individuals who gain much of the meaning and support in their lives from their networks. The result for most people is a gain of flexibility, choice and experience of heterogeneous points of view. Social ties and events are now more likely to be focused around an individual, rather than a social unit, such as a family, a neighbourhood or an organisation. People are connected directly, rather than via a social group, or via their location, whether it be home or workplace. Communications are person-to-person, rather than place-to-place, and people organise their own communications network, rather than expecting heads of households or work bosses to provide (and sometimes monitor) communication mechanisms for them.

The Web is not completely responsible for this shift, which has been a feature of the twentieth century and associated technologies such as the telephone, radio, television and mobile telephony. It has, however, exacerbated and even accelerated it. We now connect with people routinely not only at home or at the office, but at stations and in airports; furthermore, we connect with people who are not co-located with us. In fact, the physical context of a communication matters less and less.

So much is consistent with Turkle's account, but the picture might not be so bleak. People now often have *several* networks, and the tight connections that we used to expect with individuals in a single network are replaced with looser and more opportunistic connections with many others in a diverse spread of networks. The idea of a single 'home' community or identity is far less applicable. A jumble of networks is harder for the individual to manage, but pays off via the spread of services and experiences one is able to receive.

Wellman and colleagues term such people *networked individuals* [301], who have partial membership of multiple networks, rather than permanent membership of settled groups. Relationships are more transitory, but are more easily rekindled after a dormant period. The number of people reporting very close ties with family members has remained broadly stable since 1967, on Wellman's figures, while those with close ties with friends have increased in number, and those with close ties to neighbours have decreased. People reported that they had more offline friends on average in 2007 than they did in 2002, especially those who were heavy users of the Internet. Indeed, the real-world friendship networks of those heavy users not only grew quicker than any other group graded by level of Internet use, but by 2007 they were also on average larger in absolute terms than those of the other groups [368].

Households are now less like castles which allow a family to withdraw and avoid the attention of others, including the government and figures of authority, and are more like aircraft carriers, bases from which exploratory forays can be launched [185]. The house is a place where family members network with others, including work colleagues; people bring work home increasingly often. Families spend less time doing things together (including, infamously, eating dinner together at a dining table), and tend to have less of a 'family time' in common. Yet this does not mean diminishing contact; although families are together less, and parents spend less time at home, actual contact has increased over the last 20 years via the use of mobile phones in particular. A total of 35% of Canadian families feel technology has improved connections within their families, while only 5% feel it has not, as shown in the Telus Canadians and Technology survey, with some of the results reported in Ref. [375].

Indeed, ties between people seem to have become stronger, at the cost of a decrease in the perceived value of weak ties. We are less interested in strangers, and less likely to help them and care for them. Strangers are often viewed with suspicion.

Hence, even if a particular network has the problematic properties of an echo chamber that Cass Sunstein [336], Eli Pariser [286] and Turkle have identified, the chances are that its members are also members of other networks which provide support in ways other than political, ideological or religious [332]. The epistemological limitations of political discourse which concern Sunstein are arguably less dangerous in a network or Web than in more hierarchical societies. When a community is based on proximity, family and sameness of purpose, very deep communication with a small number of members is facilitated, but it is harder for new ideas and knowledge to penetrate the group. On the other hand, if someone is interacting with multiple networks and communities, they, and their networks, get exposed to new ideas all the time. Each person who is a member of more than one network connects them, or provides a bridge between them. This may provide an explanation of the oft-noted point that traditional religions are in decline alongside the fixed-proximity networks upon which they thrived, and that other religions with tighter connections, or even do-it-yourself religions, are flourishing in comparison. Such religions provide more useful benefits for networked individuals, as well as being able to communicate in more flexible ways.

Rainie and Wellman [301] identify three important revolutions which have driven the development of the networked individual. First of all there is the personal Internet revolution, which allows the individual to personalise communications, gather information and broadcast opinion. Second, there is the social network revolution, as people attach to networks rather than fix themselves within groups. Third, there is the mobile revolution, so that communications hubs can be carried around with the individual who can therefore access, and be accessible to, others at all times. Even if the Internet and Web did have a potential to seal people in echo chambers, the other two revolutions tend to counterbalance this by exposing people to new ideas.

The result is that, although people have many more relationships with people whom they know offline only slightly or not at all, they retain their relationships with their local community too. Many emails, IMs, mobile calls and texts are between locals, often supplementing face to face contacts [250]. Wellman's examination of the data shows, *contra* Turkle, that 'traditional' personal relationships seem to be supplemented, rather than replaced, by the technology. The local environment remains important, and indeed many relationships are enhanced as a result of technological mediation. People find it easier to join, rejoin and move between networks. Even if one network has an unhealthy effect on someone it does not follow that it is the only influence on the people within it. People move across and through a network of networks which widens the set of influences upon people. The Internet and the Web have not changed this — in fact they have accelerated the trend.

These considerations lead us to move from the purely local effects of a person and their immediate acquaintances and encounters. Clearly, the networks of an individual have deep effects on him or her, which may indeed be enhanced by technological mediation. We cannot understand the Web in its entirety from this narrow point of view. The macro-level effects characteristic of the Web scale require a wider perspective, which we shall introduce in the next section.

4

Patterns: The Endogenous Global

I will give out divers schedules of my beauty: it shall be inventoried, and every particle and utensil labelled to my will: as, item, two lips, indifferent red; item, two grey eyes, with lids to them; item, one neck, one chin, and so forth.

Twelfth Night, act I scene v

The emergence of patterns in the online world has been spectacularly illustrated by Candrall and colleagues [94, 386]. Working with a dataset of about 35 million geotagged images collected from Flickr, their analysis of content (via text tags and image data), and structure (via geospatial data) enabled them to uncover important relationships between the two. A 'heat map' of the dataset, where a white dot appears in the position corresponding to an image's geospatial coordinates, produces an eerily precise 'map' of the world, where those places often visited by Internet and Web users appear brightest. Without any reference to cities or coastlines, the cities and coastlines of Europe, America and East Asia are clearly interpretable by human observers. Within

Fig. 4.1 Heat map of the world from geotagged images (courtesy of the authors of Refs. [94, 386]).

particular cities, well-known features (major tourist attractions, rivers, roads, coastlines) become similarly evident merely from the pattern of locations of photos in the dataset.

The spatial distribution of where people take photos was used to define a relational structure between the photos taken at popular places. Classification methods can then predict such locations from visual, textual and temporal features of the photos. Visual and temporal features improve the ability to estimate the content of a photo, compared to using just textual tags. Crandall et al. even postulate the possibility of a guidebook automatically compiled from Flickr images. Once a map of an area has been generated, it is possible to locate the hotspots where many images have been taken, find a representative photo of that spot, and a characteristic text tag to describe the location (see also http://www.cs.cornell.edu/~crandall/photomap/).

The Web affords very large quantities of data which can deliver extraordinarily powerful descriptions of behaviour. In another instance, Song et al. [326] have shown that position data from mobile phone records can be used to predict a person's location at any time of any day with an average of 93% accuracy. The Global Epidemic and Mobility Model (GLEAM) takes data from a range of sources, including dates of school holidays and international air links, and accurately models the spread of epidemics [348, 357], while Google Flu Trends has also been celebrated for epidemiological predictions based on search terms (http://www.google.org/flutrends/). Endogenous global variables, measuring phenomena internal to the system, produce descriptions of the properties of that system as a whole. In this section, we will consider how to study the Web's macro-level properties in terms of its endogenous variables.

4.1 The Web as Graph

Perhaps the most intuitive way of looking at the Web is through the lens of discrete mathematics, as a graph, with people, machines, websites and other initiators of content as nodes, and their sociotechnical connections as vertices. More formally, a graph is a pair (V, E), where V is a set of vertices and E a set of edges (an edge being a pair of members of V; a directed edge is an ordered pair, while an undirected edge is an unordered pair). If we take the example of the Web itself, V might be the set of webpages while E would be the set of (directed) hyperlinks between the pages (although that is too neat, as it does not allow for dangling or broken links). If we take an example of a Web-based phenomenon such as SNSs, V would be the set of people, while E would be the set of friendships between people.

It is possible to model online networks as large finite graphs, and draw conclusions about the Web's properties from features that we find in the graphs. Graph and network theory are central for understanding how to spot meaningful patterns and structures in the Web.

For example, search engines exploit graph-theoretical results to extract useful content from analysis of the structure of the Web. PageRank [283] uses an approximation of a random walk method to find relevant pages. The algorithm follows hyperlinks from a random page for a particular path length, and then, in order to avoid dead ends or cycles, jumps to a new page, following links from there. The relative weight of the webpage in the distribution of this walk is its PageRank.

As the general properties of such methods are well-known, it is possible to spam search engines by artificially spoofing the structures the search algorithms are looking for (for instance by buying up defunct but well-connected pages and using those to link to others). Yet the same methods are open to use by the search engines to improve their algorithms. Anomalies can be detected and downgraded by mathematical techniques in order to blunt the spammers' weapons [15].

It would seem that graph-based theories could be used to develop methods for effective and representative sampling of the Web, but it is actually extremely hard. The Web's size and dynamism raise problems for sampling, and on top of that, there is no obvious parameter to help us understand when a sample is biased. Google's PageRank functions with a giant sample (c. 10%) of the Web, but a more complex algorithm would typically require a smaller sample where bias will be more of an issue. Borgs et al. [60, 61] have developed a graphical theory of limits, defined via graph homomorphisms, which allows the estimation of properties of large graphs, such as finding the approximate value of a parameter with associated probability, or determining whether the graph has a certain property. The limit property defined in this way has been shown to be equivalent to other well-known definitions of limits [57, 62, 63]. The result is that sampling and testing of a large graph (such as the Web, a graph so large that it cannot be completely described) can be performed with some confidence that key parameters have been preserved, and that bias can not only be defined, but also be eliminated with a determinable probability. However, applying these results in practice is still extremely hard due to the dynamic and rapidly changing nature of the Web graph.

4.2   The Web as Scale-Free Network

The Web graph is a complex network. Designed as an information network with pages/documents connected by hyperlinks, it has been treated in some detail using the methods of network science [26, 215]. On the plausible initial hypothesis that the Web is a random network in which the distribution of the degrees (i.e., the number of links to/from the nodes) of the nodes was a Poisson distribution, virtually all webpages would be close to the average degree because the Poisson declines away from the mean faster than exponentially. However, Barabási and others have shown that the Web is not random, i.e., the probability of the existence or not of a link between two nodes is not fixed.

Certain pages bring resources together in a non-random, semantically-significant way. The result is a distribution of degrees according to a power law. In 1999, it was estimated that the probability that a webpage has k links is proportional to $k^{-\gamma}$, where γ is about 2.45 for outgoing links, and about 2.1 for incoming links [9]. There are many pages with a small number of links to other pages, while a small number are immensely well-connected hubs which in effect hold the network together; using such hubs, one can quickly traverse the graph, and get from one page to another. Power law distributions decay much more slowly than other types of distributions, and so the 'average' behaviour is not very representative. A webpage with 'average' degree (a degree of about 7) will have a higher degree than most other pages, and a very much lower degree than a few well-connected pages; the fluctuations around the mean are so large that it is not a very helpful parameter. Because a typical node cannot be chosen, this is called a *scale-free* distribution [9], and in fact mirrors the structure that we find in the *physical* system of the Internet [122], in social networks, where certain people are very popular or in demand as shown by studies of email networks in Kiel University [116], and in SNSs over a range of types of connections [164]. While it is assumed that it still exhibits similar properties, the Web is now estimated to be several orders of magnitude larger than the 1999 graph, with several "dense regions" (for example, Facebook) that didn't exist at that time.

The scale-free nature of networks goes along with other important and characteristic macro-level properties, in particular the small world property [350]. Barabási and colleagues showed in 1999 that, although there were 800 m webpages at that time, one could traverse the Web in around 19 clicks [9]. More recently, the separation of people in the friendship graph of Facebook has been estimated as fewer than five degrees [25] showing both scale-free and small world properties.

The class of scale-free networks encompasses a surprising range, and it is reasonable to ask why networks, both physical and digital, formed under such different pressures, share so many structural characteristics. Barabási and Albert argued that this is because of a mechanism called *preferential attachment* [27, 53]. If we assume that the network is expanding by the addition of new nodes (in the case of the Web, new pages) which have a certain number of links, and that new nodes will tend to connect to well-connected nodes (popular sites, on the Web), then the probability that a new node will connect to a node with k links will be proportional to k. This fits in very well with our understanding of the sociotechnical nature of the Web; the creator of a webpage is likely to connect to pages of which he/she has some knowledge, and typically (a) one does not have knowledge of very many pages, and (b) one is more likely to have knowledge of well-known, well-connected hubs. Furthermore, the concept is valuable as it helps connect the micro and the macro — the pattern of links between hubs and authorities is a macro-level effect explained by the popularity of certain sites, which is an effect of an individual webpage creator being more likely to link to the ones he/she has heard of and used.

Simulations of growing networks using preferential attachment show the characteristic scale-free pattern, with a few hubs and many low-degree nodes, with a power law distribution whose exponent is sensitive to the way in which the network is growing, but is round about -3 [28]. The idea of preferential attachment accounts for the small diameter of the Web [54], the power laws associated with it, and the aging of vertices.

But more recently questions have been raised about whether the model of preferential attachment really explains the Web graph at its current scale. For example, Bollobás et al. [52] extended the preferential attachment model to describe *directed preferential attachment*, modelling the Web as a directed graph whose hyperlink/edges have a clear direction. Growth in the graph is achieved via three mechanisms. As it expands with new nodes, the new nodes will tend to link to well-connected nodes, as before. The second possibility is that a new node *will be linked to* from an existing node with a probability proportional to the out-degree of that node. The third possibility is that an old node will send an edge to another old node with a probability proportional to the out-degree of the former and the in-degree of the latter. In other words, some pages will have a stronger tendency to link to other pages, and some pages will have a stronger tendency to be linked to. Directed preferential attachment gives us different in-degree and out-degree power laws.

Preferential attachment is unlikely to be the only explanation of the growth of the Web. It tends to postulate advantage to those nodes which have been around the longest (they will have a greater opportunity to grow into hubs, and therefore to benefit from preferential attachment), but our experience of the Web tells us that this is not typical; it is quite possible for sites such as Google or Facebook to emerge from nowhere and to become important hubs. To explain this, Bianconi and Barabási [48, 49] added the idea of the *fitness* of a page, which is a measure of the tendency of other pages to link to it. The network model then argues that new pages link preferentially to pages with high degree and high fitness. If fitness is combined with preferential attachment, several phases can be discerned in the development of the graph as it grows. First, there is a first-mover-advantage phase, which corresponds to the power law behaviour predicted by the classical preferential attachment model. Secondly, there is a phase where the fit-get-richer, in which vertices of higher fitness grow faster than those of smaller fitness; the behaviour here is a power law within each fitness value, but the tail exponent decreases as the fitness increases. Finally, the graph moves towards an innovation-pays-off phase, where the competition for links results in a constant fraction of the links continuously shifting to ever larger fitness values [57, 62].

Preferential attachment can also be extended by introducing the idea of competition between opposing strategies for a node that 'wishes' to connect effectively with the rest of the graph. The node must manage a trade-off between two linking strategies; first, link to nearby nodes, which is a relatively cheap strategy, and second, link to central nodes, which is expensive but more effective in terms of establishing paths to a wider range of nodes [38]. When the nodes in a graph work to manage that trade-off, the graph grows with preferential attachment up to a certain limit, with a power law degree distribution with an exponential decay after the limit which looks more like a random network. This pattern has been shown to fit empirical data from networks in a number of areas, including technological networks such as the Internet, as well as social networks such as co-author and citation networks [110].

The resilience of a network to collapse can be studied and quantified using evidence from network structures. Garcia et al. [129] studied a series of SNSs to understand what helps them survive, and when they become vulnerable. Their sample included Friendster (http://www. friendster.com/), a site which began life in 2002 as an SNS, was one of the first SNSs to gather over a million users, was valued at $30m by Google in 2003 (the offer was turned down), but failed to keep up with the progress of MySpace and later Facebook. In 2011, its owners discontinued its social networking capabilities, and redefined it as a social gaming site. Hence Friendster is a 'failed' SNS, and as such of interest to Web Science — a discipline that only focused on the successes would struggle to provide explanations of SNSs' dynamics.

Garcia et al. [129] argued that the long-term health of any SNS depends on a cost–benefit analysis. If the costs of being a member outweigh the benefits for a long enough period of time, a person is likely to leave. If that happens, all his or her friends will have one fewer friend, thereby increasing the likelihood of those friends leaving. This process could produce a cascade of defections, which would be more or less quick, and more or less complete depending on the topological characteristics of the network. If a large proportion of the network members had two or fewer friends, then it would be vulnerable to a cascade of people leaving. Equally, if a solid proportion of people had a large number of friends, it would be less vulnerable. The fraction of the network with a threshold number of friends is called by Garcia et al. [129] the k-core distribution, and they argue that the combination of a low k-core distribution together with a negative cost–benefit distribution increases the likelihood of failure. In the case of Friendster, some argue that ill-conceived technical changes increased the costs, which meant that its low k-core distribution made it vulnerable to collapse. The cause of collapse was the change in design, but its k-core distribution was an important contributory factor.

Network models can describe more aspects of social relationships with additional expressivity. For example, Angeletou et al. [16] use semantic characteristics of roles within a network to understand its social resilience and robustness. They use rules to classify which roles particular users adopt in discussion communities, and then model their behavioural features in a generic ontology (i.e., not dependent on the particular characteristics of an individual community) in order to facilitate inferences about how robust a community is likely to be, and how changes (for instance, in the proportion or absolute number of users in particular roles) might result in the community becoming more or less robust, or simply changing function. Gathering similar resources can also support real-time analysis of communities. The Live Social Semantics initiative has studied information about communities gathering at academic conferences, including data about activities and tagging on SNSs, co-authorship networks and real-world contacts gathered using wearable sensors, to enable analyses of patterns of engagement, such as the relative networking patterns of senior and junior attenders [8, 29].

Another approach is to incorporate game theoretic ideas in which nodes are modelled as strategic agents which respond to the moves of their neighbours, trying to maximise their own utility, until an equilibrium is reached. Borgs et al. [59] have developed the 'hitch-hikers' game', in which players organise gatherings at a cost that grows with the number of attenders. That cost is assumed by the organiser but the benefit accrues equally to all attenders. A link is formed between any two players who see each other at more than a certain number of gatherings per time period, whether at gatherings organised by themselves or by third parties. Although agent utilities are locally defined, and despite its simplicity, this game nevertheless produces a rich class of Nash equilibria that exhibit structural properties commonly observed in social networks, such as triadic closure and other types of clustering that do not appear in simpler or more structurally based models. The graphs produced exhibit much richer structures than the cliques or trees that game theoretic models tend to produce.

The value of network models to understand the Web seems clear. However, it is worth treating them with some caution — an examination from the perspective of theoretical ecology has argued that insights from what is understood about networks in ecological contexts and their dynamical properties can be extended to an understanding of systemic risk in communities of networked elements, for example, in the banking system [233]. This understanding of real world network phenomenology leads to a number of caveats about our assumptions with respect to Web structure. The Web may not be altogether "scale-free", in the sense that we cannot assume that a sample from a network is representative of the network's degree distribution. The challenge is to know how to sample the Web so as to meet these conditions. Even if the degree distribution is accurately known, it does not fully characterise the network. Furthermore, in many contexts a network's dynamic response to a disturbance will depend not only on its topology, but also on the strengths of, or flows along, individual links.

4.3   The Web as Enabler of the Network Society

Conceptualising the Web as a network in the mathematical sense provides a point of contact with the social sciences, where the Web is seen as a key technological enabler of a series of developments which collectively have led to the coining of the term 'the network society' [82, 83, 84]. This concept, developed by Castells, extends the idea, familiar since the work of Bell [33] in the 1970s, of the post-industrial society, and the even more venerable predictions of Young [385] about the rise of the meritocracy. Bell argued that patterns of development were visible which created a whole new set of conditions. In business, there was a shift from manufacturing to services. Meanwhile, science was becoming a stronger driver of technology, and socially the rise of technical elites (who were capable of defending their social gains, leading to the entrenched meritocracy that Young predicted) became evident. This led to a vision of social evolution, from a pre-industrial, agricultural period, to an industrial period characterised by mass production and manufactures, leading eventually to the post-industrial age characterised by services and information industries.

This vision is compelling in a number of ways, but only if one focuses on particular sectors and particular countries. It is a vision with a specific basis in trends in the United States (Bell was generally clear on this, but those who followed him were not always). US-centrism can be a problem with research in this sort of area — Milgram's small world experiments in the 1960s also suffered from what we might call the 'World Series Baseball' assumption that the US is (representative of) the whole world. A number of commentators have criticised Bell's thesis as too vague, ethnocentric and selective [372].

Castells' ideas have been deliberately cast more widely, focusing on developments across the globe in a range of economic sectors and levels of technological development, also including analysis of those refuseniks who challenge globalisation and other economic trends [84, pp. 71–167]. His focus is on the use of information in social development, rather than postulating the specific boundaries and conceptual changes of post-industrialism (he avoids talk of a pre-information age which the information age has ended). Such concessions are not enough for some commentators who resist all definitions of an information age (e.g., [372]) as attempting to place too much emphasis on one type of social change and ignoring other trends, while Castells' individual view has also been criticised in a number of quarters [130]. For our purposes, we do not need to take a position on this dispute within social science — all we need note from the Web Science perspective is that there are many thinkers who are prepared to conduct the sociology of information and information use [373], which is clearly a relevant discipline.

Informationalism, as Castells calls the paradigm, is a mode of development, not a mode of production like capitalism. A mode of development is a technical term for Castells, meaning a technological arrangement through which labour works on objects to create products, whether for direct consumption or for surplus (and therefore trade). In the informational mode, the technologies of knowledge generation, information processing and symbolic communication are the mainstays of the creation of economic value. In particular, knowledge acts upon knowledge, and is applied in order to increase the quantity and complexity of knowledge accumulated [82, pp. 77–162]. He links the emergence of informationalism to a restructuring of the capitalist mode of production at the end of the twentieth century. In technological terms, the Internet and the Web are cornerstones of this social pattern, and specific attempts to drive the Web's development (e.g., the Semantic Web and open data, discussed in Section 6.2) can be understood very straightforwardly as tools for the informational mode of development where knowledge is accumulated and aggregated, and where possible made available for anyone to use in order to increase the number of serendipitous contexts in which it can be applied. The anticipated results are precisely the decentralised improvement of knowledge generation and information processing that Castells postulates.

In a framing device recalling structuration as well as Figure 2.1, he writes that "our societies are increasingly structured around a bipolar opposition between the Net and the self" [82, p. 3]. This opposition speaks to the Web Science concerns of emergence and the complex causal interactions between the micro and the macro. Castells detects a series of strategies of identity-creation, ranging from social movements, religious fundamentalism, opposition to globalisation and so on [84]. He sees a general phenomenon of people creating or fostering identities to counteract the growth of the network society, focusing on the local or the resistant. As the networks in societies grow, and societies begin to merge [308], there is a feeling of exclusion — quite possibly related to the alienation discussed in Section 3.3 above [352] — which begets the reaction of localised identity. In Web Science terms, many questions are raised about technological affordances, and how far identity makes sense in inclusionary rather than exclusionary terms. Can there be such a thing as the global citizen? How does the extraordinary success of SNSs affect Castells' general thesis? How do people feel about their use of Facebook (say), in which their interactions are (intended to be) with individuals of their acquaintance, however remote, but where their data, the raw material of identity, is the property of Facebook, and may be used in all sorts of ways to constrain choice and narrow their range of experience?

Castells does have a radical political agenda [85, 86], supporting "the social movements of the network society . . . that will ultimately make societies in the twenty-first century by engaging in conflictive practices rooted in the fundamental contradictions of our world." He does this "with the hope of identifying the new paths of social change in our time" [86, p. 4]. As should be clear from Section 1 of this monograph, Web Science with its engineering focus is neither committed nor opposed to this agenda, but Castells' pioneering sociological work is valuable independently of his normative political thesis.

4.4 The Dark Web

Like all societies, the network society has its dark side. Castells writes that "criminal activities and Mafia-like organizations around the world have also become global and informational, providing the means for stimulation of mental hyperactivity and forbidden desire, along with all forms of illicit trade demanded by our societies, from sophisticated weaponry to human flesh" ([82, p. 2] and see [83, pp. 169–211] for detailed analysis). Two of the most important transformations that the Web has made in the area of crime are the empowerment of the individual, allowing lone offenders to use the power of networks to carry out tasks of unprecedented complexity (and to repeat them many times rapidly), and the affordances for groups or coalitions to form and unform [367]. It is unsurprising that the same affordances that support legal or compulsory behaviour can also be applied to make behaviour that is forbidden or discouraged both easier to carry out and harder to detect or prevent (for a troubling example, see [92]).

The Web alters the balance of incentives for individuals as well as empowering them. Hence it will change local action [4, 5]. But new patterns also emerge at the macro-level. Moura's PhD thesis [259] is a survey of how 'bad behaviour' is distributed over the Internet — even though most attacks and criminal behaviour come from across the Internet, network analyses show how to calculate the probability of a host being part of the dark Web based on the incidence of malfeasance across neighbours (other hosts in the same subnetwork). In fact, malicious hosts can be traced at varying levels of abstraction — for instance, Moura discovered that, out of over 42,000 ISPs investigated, 20 contained almost half of all spamming IP addresses. In one ISP, 62% of all its IP addresses were involved with spam. Some bad neighbourhoods were application-specific, and some were geographically correlated — for instance, phishing attacks tended to come from the United States and other developed nations. And although individual IP addresses were relatively unlikely to host repeat attacks against the same victims, repeats were very likely to come from the same bad neighbourhoods [259].

In a series of papers, Yip et al. [383, 384] have investigated how structures of networks enable or facilitate cybercrime, by looking at empirical evidence taken from carding forums (secure forums where stolen data and related goods and services are traded) through various lenses, including social psychology, the criminology of organised crime and transaction cost economics. Such evidence becomes available with a time lag — only when a forum such as Carderplanet or ShadowCrew is closed down can the data about the network be harvested. This data is both qualitative — the content of the forum messages, for instance — and quantitative — such as the numbers of messages passed between various actors. Yip et al. [384] argue that many aspects of the forums have been designed in order to mitigate the various types of uncertainty inherent in illegal enterprise. Criminals are unlikely to possess spotless reputations for trustworthiness, and even when they do, there is a significant risk that a pseudonymous person on a carding forum, accessible only virtually, is a policeman.

Hence a pattern emerges of carding forums as promoters of trust. Merely being in contact with other cybercriminals is not sufficient for a market to develop [159] — the market needs a tangible online 'place' and structures. Yip et al. argue that although a network is an ideal structure for efficient information flow, the lack of trust and the constant dampening effect of mistrust mean that elements of hierarchy are needed to lower transaction costs — these elements are there for administrative and regulatory purposes, not to coordinate the network members or allocation of resources. The forum provides coordination and social networking services, as well as mitigating uncertainty about trustworthiness and also about the quality of the merchandise [383]. As far as policing is concerned, this sort of multilevel and interdisciplinary analysis is important for determining what trust signals a law enforcement agent would have to send in order to pose successfully as a cybercriminal who could command trust from his 'peers' [384].

These discoveries help suggest specific counter-measures — for instance, looking at ISPs would appear to be a promising approach for detecting spam emails. They point up the importance of getting the right data for understanding the patterns that emerge from the action of many individuals, which brings us onto the important topic of how to collect and to disseminate that data.

4.5 Instrumenting the Web: The Web Observatory

The need for the right data to understand the emergent phenomena of the Web was discussed briefly in Section 2.1. Understanding the patterns to be seen in the Web at the macro-scale, which appear as the result of many instances of local action, requires data. Data is collected on the Web from a number of sources, including SNSs, clickthroughs on websites and so on. But there is also a need for data on how the Web develops as a technological network and on how the networks of people that engage in social machines emerge and shape its evolution. Data must be supplemented by qualitative and quantitative methodologies and tools to better foster the research of the Web as a network of networks.

There is of course more to the Web than this. It is increasingly an archive of human activity. Developments in the world are continuously reported on resources available on the Web as blogs, news reports, stock exchange data, geo-tagged and time-stamped resources. As should be clear by now, the Web is not only a shaper but also a reflection of human activity. Hence, it is multi-faceted, a lens onto the networks that use it (whether wider society, specific social networks or specific activities, such as scientific research), an infrastructure for data distribution and analysis, and an artefact in its own right. Instrumenting it comprehensively would provide many different kinds of data.

A number of academic resources and repositories are being developed or are in operation, some using specific techniques for gathering data (e.g., [262]) and others collecting specific types of data (e.g., [177, 239]), and coordinating these could produce an observatory of the Web. A Web Observatory will only arrive once institutions begin to encourage interoperability and standardisation. Specific projects naturally have their own internal priorities, but to the extent that they can be seen against the background of a wider drive to understand the macro-level patterns of the Web, we begin to see more clearly how to bring data together for a wider view. The following processes and capabilities seem key to the development of a Web Observatory [71]:

- Exchanges of data between collaborating partners, on the basis of formal agreements or terms and conditions. The data will not necessarily be open data, and there may be a charging model for access, a licensing agreement and a description of permitted use of the data.

- Specification of the provenance of the data, and a formal classification of the data.
- Communication across repositories, with discovery of sources, disclosure of metadata and the granting of licences.
- Queries would be made in the context of a specific research question, which implies specific methods, tools, commentary and collaboration to address them.
- No site to hold all the data. Each partner would be engaged in regular collection of data, with metadata to support validation and format conversion.
- Datasets constructible from multiple sources.
- Choreographed updating. Curation processes such as selection, deletion, annotation, classification and reclassification, especially of automatically-harvested data, must be carried out.

Furthermore, some data would naturally be extremely sensitive. boyd and Crawford [66] not only talk of SNSs as being "living labs", providing access to behavioural data at unprecedented scales (cf. also [2, 108, 109, 191, 241]), but also draw attention to the serious ethical implications and the need to be alert to the potential introduction of new types of biases. Ellison and boyd [118] also point out that the sociotechnical context of any particular (analysis of a) dataset will change rapidly, and that many studies of online practices are outdated by the time they are published (cf. [273]). This will also affect comparisons between and aggregations of data collected at different times, and will have implications for the data collected for longitudinal studies. The Truthy system [239, 240, 241], a system which collects Twitter data to analyse discourse within communication networks, and the Friends and Family study, a longitudinal living laboratory with rich data based on smartphones and sensors [2], are important data-gathering exercises that have had to address these issues.

The Web Observatory (http://thewebobservatory.org) project coordinated by the Web Science Trust (http://webscience.org/WSTNet.html) is working to facilitate the collection, harmonisation and dissemination of data resources for the study of the Web on a global collaborative basis based on the properties listed above [347]. Similarly, interdisciplinary research methods are required, as well as tools and interactive visualisations [241]. The Web Observatory is intended to empower Web Scientists to enrich and expand their research by providing a collection of new and existing data sources and analytic tools. A W3C community group on Web Observatories (http://www.w3.org/community/webobservatory) fosters discussion on standardisation to assist integration. The Web Observatory as it develops is intended to support both applied and core research, by laying bare the macro-level patterns of the Web, and their links with the micro-level behaviour that causes the former to emerge [147, 347].

5

Feedback: The Exogenous Local

The heart of brothers govern in our loves
And sway our great designs!

Antony and Cleopatra, act II scene ii

When the macro emerges from the micro, large-scale phenomena establish causal influence with the individuals from whose behaviour they have emerged. High-level phenomena change the behaviour of individuals, whose small-scale environment is affected by variables at the network scale beyond their control. For instance, many individuals make decisions to buy goods or not; sometimes these decisions collectively produce large-scale phenomena such as inflation; inflation will then influence decisions to buy in the future. Here, local effects need to be understood in terms of variables exogenous to the local environment (though still within the system).

The Web furnishes an opportunity for sociologists and social scientists. Social interactions now leave traces, and basic patterns identifying those interactions can be uncovered using number-crunching algorithms on very large quantities of data, thereby bypassing the problems caused by the poor signal-to-noise ratio [22, 234].

These considerations illuminate the relationship between online and offline life. Consider how, for example, Milgram's small world discovery causes us to pose the question of how people can find the short chains traversing their own networks. In the real world, or even in a non-abstract, though online, setting like Facebook, no doubt there are navigational cues undetectable by number crunching on large datasets. However, theoretical analysis can tell us *under what conditions* short chain detection would even be possible with only local knowledge (e.g., Kleinberg 2008). This consideration brings together representations of local actions with the global activity of spotting macro-level patterns on the Web.

It is an open question as to how important these results are for society as a whole. Rainie and Wellman [301] argue that, as more people live more of their lives, and have more significant interactions, online, these technical results become more significant. Those opposing this view do not necessarily dispute the major premise that online life does constitute a larger share of human and social interaction, and that therefore the empirical results obtained by analysing graphs and networks using data gathered online are valid about at least a significant (and probably increasing) fraction of human interaction. The question is how much the study of online behaviour tells you about offline behaviour [346]. Behaviour offline may be very different from online behaviour, although (a) one might anticipate that these would grow closer over time as social norms emerge in communities well-versed in online *mores*, and (b) online behaviour constitutes an ever-greater proportion of behaviour as a whole.

Kleinberg has argued that online data can help answer longstanding sociological questions, such as (i) what the probability is of forming new friendships or engaging in new activities based on the behaviour of existing friends [23, 30, 140, 199, 206, 309]), (ii) whether similarity with friends follows convergence with friends' attitudes and behaviour, or whether one seeks friendships with like-minded and socially-similar people [13, 17, 95]), and (iii) how positive and negative evaluations propagate through a social network [208, 209, 339]. The numbers of people who can be studied in offline interactions tend to be very low, which makes it hard to distinguish between different theories (e.g., whether people are affected by a 'critical mass' of friends, and if so what that critical mass is), whereas online studies on large datasets make it possible to formulate and test theories meaningfully. Nevertheless, as Kleinberg himself points out assiduously, we should be wary of taking the parallels too far [191]; the large-scale data analysis which the Web facilitates is complementary to, and does not replace, smaller-scale qualitative analyses of offline behaviour. The aim of Web Science is to build systems that enable and empower human behaviour — not to change human behaviour, although equally one might expect that as certain formerly offline interactions migrate online, their nature may change in time as new methods of expression and new species of connection become available.

5.1 Content

The Web is distinguished from other media because of the potential for asynchronous multi-way communication among many participants. As Dutton [114, p. 5] puts it, "users can choose to open themselves to a greater plurality of messages, or create an 'echo chamber' to reinforce their preconceived views. They can create content, be more passive consumers, or create in a diverse range of activities that fall short of the full potential that the Internet enables". The Web (a) brings non-technical and non-professional users to the Internet, (b) provides the protocols that made the diversity that Dutton identifies possible, and (c) bridges the training gaps and digital divides that could have prevented the democratisation of online content creation. Elton and Carey [121] provide a historical survey of the precursors to the Web, and argue that much of the Web's functionality, such as online banking, news, commentary and discussions, had already appeared in various standalone applications or in technologies such as Videotex systems (Minitel and Prestel) which had accustomed their user bases to important types of interaction. In particular, the experience of these technologies demonstrated the importance of content provision and conversation (unidirectional communication rarely succeeded, and interaction was often important), and showed how open systems were generally more successful than walled gardens. Yet important as those precursors were, it is clear from this account that the technologies of the Internet and the Web dramatically increased usage by overcoming the obstacles to wide uptake that characterised the earlier efforts.

The competitive advantage of the Web is that it provides immediate and interesting feedback to content creators — and indeed much of the content on the Web actually is direct feedback to other creators. In this subsection, we will survey research into the role of content in understanding the dynamics of the Web. Who produces, or consumes, what, and why?

5.1.1   Analyses of Content Provision

Chan and Hayes classified users of a bulletin board which incorporates a wide-ranging and potentially interesting set of measures and classes[88]. They defined a series of features: structural features measuring communications between users; reciprocity features, measuring the likelihood of a connection being bidirectional; persistence features, measuring the length of discussions; popularity features, measuring the number and range of replies a user receives; and initialisation features, measuring the number of threads that a user initiates. Based on these, Chan and Hayes clustered the users of an Irish bulletin board semi-automatically to define types such as 'popular participants', who are involved with a large percentage of forum users, but do not initiate many threads, or 'grunts', who communicate rarely but often reciprocate communications [88].

Different forums had very different profiles. The Christianity forum was made up of 55% supporters (broadly middle of the road in all the statistics), 31% popular participants, 11% grunts and 3% popular initiators (initiate a lot of threads, and are involved with a large percentage of users); the martial arts forum was made up of 55% grunts, 36% supporters, 7% taciturns (low reciprocity, low volume of communications and few neighbours) and 2% popular participants; while the travel forum was made up of 78% taciturns and 22% grunts. There were also similarities between certain types of forum in terms of their make-up of these types of participant, so forums themselves could be clustered too. For example, 'travel' looked like 'gigs & events'; 'accommodation' looked like 'politics'.

There have been a number of analyses along similar lines, using methodologies based on clustering on local factors, so there is no commonly agreed set of behaviour patterns and labels. However, some commonalities of significant social and technical features have emerged, even if only relative to the online communities under investigation. Users who contribute with high intensity, reciprocity and a focus on contributing to the community and keeping discussion going are a particularly important group, whether they are classified as popular initiators, moderators, celebrities [138], captains [296] or pillars [334]. Those who make little positive contribution also form common groups, attracting pejorative names like grunts, taciturns, content consumers [226] or lurkers [138, 296, 334]. Angeletou et al. [16] attempt a more principled and synthetic categorisation of such roles in online discussion communities based on parameters such as the number of threads initiated, the average number and standard deviation of posts per thread, and the in-degree of a person in the network (calculated as the number of network members who have replied to his posts). Recent work on microblogging has produced similar analyses, including categories like 'super spreaders,' who generate significantly more tweets than others, and 'rapid retweeters,' who provide almost instant retweets (many of which are automated 'tweetbots,' further complicating the analyses) [56, 171, 172, 222, 333].

Lim et al. [219] define a *content power user* in the blogosphere as a person who is influential in the sense of inducing activities in the blog network by other users, and aim to suggest ways in which influence can be manifested, including static behaviours such as bookmarking and dynamic behaviours. They focus on the latter, especially reproductive behaviours like trackbacking. They compute the *content power* of a document in terms of the activities and behaviours of other users that are influenced by the document, especially behaviours that involve reproduction of the original document. A user's content power is calculated by summing the content power of all the documents he owns, normalised to remove the effects of time (a document which has been published for longer is more likely to influence others than a more recent one).

Lim et al. performed an experimental evaluation on a Korean blog network of over 100m documents in 2006, which produced interesting results. Of course there was no gold standard of accuracy, but they did compare against other methods of computing influence. The distribution of influence, as with other methods, produced graphs looking like power functions (a small number of users with large influence). However, the actual sets of users identified were quite dissimilar; the users identified by Lim et al.'s method had more of their documents linked to by others, which seems to indicate that their method improved on straightforward network analysis in terms of identifying influence. Finally, depending on the weightings involved, Lim et al.'s method shows change over time, so after a period of 90–120 days, about 35–40% of the power users were different. This was much greater churn than with analyses using other methods, implying that their method was sensitive to the dynamics of the blogosphere.

Letierce et al. [213] looked at the use of Twitter within three events (the 2009 International Semantic Web Conference, Online09, and the 2009 European Semantic Technology Conference), crawling all messages with the hashtag of the conference from a few days before each conference began. Using the HITS algorithm [190], they looked for hubs and authorities — i.e., authorities receiving lots of tweets with the @user patter, hubs sending them — and discovered that the organisers of the conferences were both hubs and authorities, unsurprisingly. Those with authority in the community, or within the event (keynote speakers, for instance) were also hubs and authorities. A relatively large proportion (20%) of tweets were retweets. Spikes in the numbers of tweets sent correlated with events such as awards ceremonies, the appearance of an article in the *New York Times* about linked data, and popular keynotes. The deliberate use of the conference hashtag showed that users were keen to be associated with it, and to be read in that context; other hashtags used in the same tweets tended to be technical ones, again aimed at the community rather than the media, say, or the wider non-scientific community. Most included hyperlinks were to papers, presentations or other pieces of technical documentation.

Retweets tended to be about projects related to the retweeter (as discovered by interviews afterwards). In general, users attending these meetings largely wished to communicate with their own community, and specifically the people in the room. There was little effort to reach out to wider communities.

This compares to Ref. [141], which used standard bibliometrics, usually used to analyse academic papers, to look at scientific blogs, and to compare them with more formal publications in the field of chemistry. In particular, they looked at keyword and citation similarity maps to map the blogosphere in chemistry. The blogs in question were not self-selected, but selected via quality criteria using researchblogging.org, an aggregator. They discovered that scientific discourse on the Web is more immediate. Older publications are less likely to share topics with more recent publications, and are more likely to be isolated, while new blog posts tend to refer to recent publications. Scientific discourse on the Web is also more contextually relevant, as blogs are more likely to refer back to classic papers or other scene-setting materials. The blog discourse also focuses on high quality science, tending to refer to papers in higher-impact journals than scientific papers. Yet it also focuses on non-technical implications. Analysis of words used shows a larger number of subnetworks and dispersed topics. The upshot of the last two analyses is that producers of tweets and blogs have, unsurprisingly, different aims and criteria for success, even in similar domains.

Szabo and Huberman [338] argue that there are different patterns to the popularity of Web 2.0 posts depending on how long the post has been active. They show that, at least with Digg and YouTube, they can predict with some accuracy how popular a post will be after several days, given its performance in the first few hours of posting. They also show that, although social networking effects are important in these early stages, ultimately, when a post becomes very popular, it builds up its own momentum and the effects of the network become negligible. Even so, this leaves open the possibility that in Web 2.0 sites such as these, carefully nurtured influence in the early stages can lead to a story spreading. When a story is placed in Digg, fans of the person who dug the story are disproportionately likely to digg it in the early stages. If these fans manage to get the story promoted to the front page, then it will get access to a far wider group of people. The site was redesigned in 2012 in response to concerns that groups were manipulating the front page [281].

Safran and Kappe [307] looked for success factors in a blogging community, where success was measured as the number of hits from different IP addresses. Obviously this is not equivalent to influence, but we might expect a correlation between popularity and influence [338]. Safran and Kappe found nine of their hypotheses confirmed, with success factors ranging from aspects of presentation of content, to social behaviour, to writing style. Authors were more likely to attract more visitors if they (a) wrote more posts, (b) provided more images, (c) provided new content more often, (d) actively commented on other blogs, (e) actively posted in others' guestbooks and (f) mimicked the writing style of mass media journalists.

5.1.2　Analyses of Content Consumption

There has been a lot of research on content provision, but somewhat less on the roles, motivations and susceptibility of content consumers. One study of political blogs [123] tries to explain the mystery of why blogs are influential at all, given that hardly anyone reads them (compared to the numbers that read newspapers or watch the television). It focuses, as many authors do, on the power laws of the blogosphere, where the median blogger has virtually no influence at all, while a few blogs are enormously well-connected. However, many blog readers are not just readers; the key readers of the influential blogs will spread ideas, and therefore are likely to be amplifiers, curators or commentators either in the same network, or in other networks of influence (e.g., the mass media). Someone may be very influential in a domain, thanks to a presence in a particular medium, even though they are not very active in that medium. Although only 7% of the public read political blogs, 83% of journalists did, and 43% read them at least weekly [123]. This helps explain the otherwise surprising influence of political blogs (at least in the US, where the research was performed).

Furthermore, as experiments reported in Refs. [31] and [225] highlight, the roles of would-be opinion formers can be delineated not only via their positions in the network, but also via their place in the wider context. In her study of PR interventions using new media, Bates argued that journalists perceived as independent of a company were taken by readers to be more credible than PR people associated with the company (as one would expect). However, it also turned out that the responses on a blog affected readers' perceptions of credibility both of the PR bloggers and the companies they were trying to support; largely positive comments increased the positive perception of PR bloggers' credibility. Her conclusion is that, in order to maximise positive perceptions (an important influence criterion), it is useful to attract readers to the company blog before any crisis happens, to maximise the likelihood that they are exposed to positive comments [31]. Mack et al. [225] discovered in the tourism industry that, although word-of-mouth was reliably perceived as more credible than tourism companies' own blogs, the companies' blogs were perceived as more authoritative as information sources, and so there is a distinct type of credibility relative to which PR or advertising could have some sort of advantage.

Hindman [163] reports an informal survey of top political bloggers in the US. Using traffic from December 2004 as a baseline, Hindman gathered information on every political blog that averaged over 2000 visitors per week, to create a list of 87 blogs, and then gathered background information on about 75 of their authors. They were a very unrepresentative group. A total of 64% had been to an elite educational institution (an Ivy League university or other prominent university, or a top military service academy or liberal arts college); 61% had a higher degree; 20% were lawyers; 25% were or had been college professors; 21% were journalists; 37% were top business people (serving on the board, being senior management consultants, or serving in senior strategic management roles); and 39% were technologists. When compared to top op-ed columnists in newspapers, the top bloggers were a much more elite group, and because of the Matthew effect that the rich get richer, characteristic of the scale-free Web, the top bloggers hogged a far greater percentage of online traffic than the op-ed journalists were able to manage in the traditional mass media.

5.2   Influence

The skewed nature of the blogosphere can help coordinate writers and readers. We can think of blogging as a coordination game, where writers and readers each wish to reach an equilibrium via cooperation, and they are not too particular which equilibrium they choose. Bloggers wish to maximise readership but have difficulties finding new readers because the space is very crowded. Readers wish to find interesting blog posts, which gives them a search problem. Hence a small number of influential blogs can help both types of participant. Bloggers can contact large blogs hoping they will link back to the original post, in which case they can gain new readers. Meanwhile the large blogs act as filters or editors of the large blog space.

Yeung [381] has studied strategies for content consumers to exploit other users, in effect using them as information filters. His question is not how a site should present information, but what information should the consumer be looking for to find what he wants (not necessarily the most popular items, of course). In his study of the bookmarking site deli.cio.us, Yeung examines a series of strategies that make sense for the consumer: follow active users (i.e., users that have adopted a lot of items); follow users with many followers; follow predecessors (i.e., users who adopted items that the consumer later adopted); follow like-minded users (i.e., using collaborative filtering). Note that only the last two can be personalised to a particular consumer. He discovered that following active users was particularly efficacious in presenting users with items that interested them sooner than other strategies; the reason for this is perhaps that following active users presents the consumer with a diverse range of options. Following predecessors is more effective at uncovering content quickly than following similar neighbours. In this context, it is worth also thinking about motivation for blog readers. Based on an admittedly non-random survey, [183] isolates nine motivational factors for prompting people to read blogs; convenient information provision, and anti-traditional media sentiment were about as important as the other seven combined.

Crandall et al. [95] found that influence spreads through populations who become more similar to each other. However, similarity affects different domains in different ways. In Wikipedia, mutual influence was more common when people worked together on particular projects, whereas on LiveJournal similarity between people was more a predictive factor for future behaviour. Crandall et al. drew the conclusion that hybrid approaches to recommendations, taking into account both similarity and the history of social interactions, should be fruitful; in each of the cases they studied this would have brought extra information into consideration of future action.

5.2.1 Mechanisms of Influence

There are a number of mechanisms for influence. For example, there is *fashion*: A performs some action; A is admired by B for some reason; and so B copies A. Another example is *informing*: A tells B about something, which convinces B to act in some particular way. A third example is *networking*: the more people perform some action, the more value B can get out of it (Metcalfe's Law, the network effect). A fourth is *word of mouth*, which is a combination of informing and networking. Clearly, these mechanisms have different properties, and demand different relationships between A and B. Rowe et al. [306] used an analysis of the roles that people adopt in discussion networks (see also [16]) to predict the course of discussions, in particular trying to identify seed posts which will provoke a lot of discussion, and estimating the level of discussion that will follow.

Aral and Walker [18] discovered in a study of Facebook that, at large scale, the network structure of influence has a certain signature. In an experiment using data about the take-up of a product on the basis of recommendations they looked at how influential individuals are, and how susceptible they are to influence, and also how these relate to their position in the network. Aran and Walker were able to show that influence and susceptibility did not tend to go together — influencers were less often influenced by others. Furthermore, influential people clustered together in the network to a greater extent than the noninfluential, which implies that the most important factor in influence is the existence of a group of influential friends acting in concert.

Yamamoto and Matsumura [379] have shown that the optimal conditions for word of mouth demand a recommender who knows only slightly more than the receiver, and whose influence is slightly greater than the receiver. Their study showed that the influence of an elite few was less than often assumed, and that there are a large number of what they call 'grassroots influentials' whose influence is more easily found, more likely to be sought and more likely to be acted upon. This is perhaps worrying in the context of discoveries like that by Davies et al. [97] that antivaccination sites appeared prominently in Google searches for terms like 'vaccination' and 'immunization', and that such sites tended to use highly rhetorical strategies and conspiracy theories for the purposes of persuading their readers. Davies and his colleagues concluded that "There is a high probability that parents will encounter elaborate antivaccination material on the World Wide Web. Factual refutational strategies alone are unlikely to counter the highly rhetorical appeals that shape these sites."

We should also note that technology changes the type of interaction allowed, and therefore the type of influence supported; for example an important development is mobile communication [182]. Twitter now allows real-time commenting on, say, a presentation while it is going on, while applications such as Yelp (http://www.yelp.com/) thrive on the real-time element. This has been transformative. For instance, while the first debate between the 2012 US Presidential Election candidates Barack Obama and Mitt Romney was still underway, Twitter was already generating a narrative of Obama's relative and unexpected failure, rejuvenating Romney's faltering campaign. In the second debate, an unwise comment of Romney's to the effect that he had collected "binders full of women" produced a powerful meme, complete with animated gifs, across the Web before the debate had finished. Where the story of the 2008 election was the influence of blogs, microblogging seemed to have taken over by 2012 [272].

The increase in influence of such technologies will tend to increase the preponderance of recycled ideas; after all, a tweet (and more obviously a retweet) depends on speed and reaction rather than consideration and reflection. Similarly, Metaxas and Mustafaraj's [246] study of the 2010 Senate race in Massachusetts shows the distortion of traditional patterns of influence by a newly launched technology. "Recently, all major search engines introduced a new feature: real-time search results, embedded in the first page of organic search results. The content appearing in these results is pulled within minutes of its generation from the so-called 'real-time Web' such as Twitter, blogs, and news websites. ... In the context of political speech, this feature provides disproportionate exposure to personal opinions, fabricated content, unverified events, lies and misrepresentations that otherwise would not find their way in the first page, giving them the opportunity to spread virally."

Note also that capacity for influence depends on the size of a community [280]. Large and small networks have fundamentally different properties from each other because in a small network the individual contribution can be tracked, thereby introducing the notion of responsibility and lowering the potential for free riding. When networks begin to scale, we should expect underprovision of public goods. When the individual contribution of a content provider can be tracked, and rewarded more easily, the implication of Olson [280] is that proportionately more providers will provide diverse information services, so that in the smaller network the categories of providers may well be more fluid. Someone might be an idea starter today and a curator tomorrow. In a larger network, however, one would expect more free riding (i.e., more readers), and fewer public goods, proportionately. This has the advantage that it improves search; identification of hubs lowers the overheads on the discovery and dissemination of ideas.

5.2.2 Influence on the Basis of Topic and Sentiment

Many approaches to influence also examine the importance of topic and sentiment. Szabo and Huberman [338] argue that with a large population, accurate predictions of future popularity of posted content can be made from knowing the pattern of initial data concerning popularity in the first hours or days after it is posted (the exact relevant timescales depend on the application; with Digg the important time is extremely short, while with YouTube there is a longer relevant period). However, when the populations are smaller, it is necessary to look at the semantics of the post to get a sense of how popular it will be.

Topic analysis need not be very sophisticated to be of value. Degirmencioglu and Uskudarli [101] use a simple key word extraction algorithm to determine topics within Twitter, and use these to cluster communities of interest. They argue that this simple method, based as it is on user contribution, is of more use in topic classification than either self-classification or popularity measures.

Song et al. [327] define a function InfluenceRank, loosely modelled on PageRank, to rank blogs not only according to their importance relative to other blogs, but also how novel is the information they contribute to the network. It takes inspiration from PageRank's assumption that the importance of a webpage is proportional to the importance of the pages that link to it, and also the idea behind HITS [190] that good hubs point to good authorities, and good authorities are pointed to by good hubs.

What the method of Song et al. hopes to add to these network-based ideas is the possibility of identifying novel content. So, for example, if blog A creates some new idea (a criticism of a particular piece of software, say), then it might be referred to by blog B, and we can straightforwardly say that A has influenced B. However, suppose blog C also refers to or reproduces the content of A, but in a new context; for example, C is talking about the likely future effects on the share price of a firm which produces the software. In that case, C has introduced a new idea, but it has also reproduced the argument of A which is relevant to its argument. C is therefore influenced by A, but is different from B because it is also an opinion leader as it introduced a new idea. How can we detect this distinction?

Most work in topic detection looks at document streams, and does not take account of the non-linear linking structures that are needed to understand the blogosphere. Song et al. model the creation of new information by adding a new, hidden, node to the network, which links to an existing node and represents the capacity for novel information produced by that node. The information produced by a blog can then be traced back either to another blog to which it is linked, or, if the information is new to the network, to the hidden node. In the example above, the criticism of the software made in C would be traced back eventually to blog A, while the inference about the share price of the company would be allocated to the fictitious hidden node.

Yeung et al. [382] have also tried to refine the notion of expertise in collaborative tagging systems, to try to go beyond the HITS hub and authority model, and have suggested a similar approach to InfluenceRank which they call SPEAR. In their study of the bookmarking site deli.cio.us, they connect the definition of an expert not only with the documents he tags, but also (a) with the *quality* of those documents (experts find better documents), and (b) with their *novelty* (experts find them sooner, and with less aid from the rest of the community).

As noted above, Degirmencioglu and Uskudarli [101] use a simple keyword scheme to discover topics of tweets. In a similar spirit, Backstrom et al. [23] analyse topics, conferences and author behaviour, using data from LiveJournal and DBLP and taking words in paper titles as indicators of topics. Their analyses are wide-ranging and interesting, enabling them to track the growth, decline and merging of conferences and how they affect and are affected by author behaviour. For instance, they were able to discover that when a conference grows, so that more new authors gravitate towards it, the new authors' papers tend to be about disproportionately 'hot' topics (i.e., topics which have grown in popularity over the last time period). However, these authors tend not to bring influential new ideas with them, and seem to be following trends; their papers tend not to be related to topics which are not currently hot, but which will become hot in the next time period.

More complex methods are also available. The calculation of information novelty used by Song et al. [327] uses a method called Latent Dirichlet Allocation (LDA), which exploits co-occurrence patterns of words in documents to find semantically significant clusters of words which can then be grouped into topics. Then documents can be assigned probabilities for their membership of particular topics in the topic space, depending on how many of the key words of each topic occur in it, and how frequently. This method of topic identification is common, but as pointed out by Nallapati and Cohen [261], ignores the important additional information that a blog that is influenced by another blog is relatively likely to be about related topics. Their measure of topicality follows standard methods in being able to express the fact that a document is influential in a topic when other documents in the same topic refer or link to it, but they go further by being able to express the relevance of the topics in a particular document to the topics in a user's query. In other words, their method gives a handle on not only the relation of documents to the topic space, but also the structure of the topic space itself. In the past couple of years, LDA has become a standard way of exploring topics on microblogs as it is well suited to the short documents.

The use of topics allows further sensitivity in the measurement of influence by detecting sentiment and opinion, on the assumption that influence counts more when it is positive. Kale et al. [179] represent an influence graph as a connected series of edges with a vector of the topic responsible for the influence, and a weight representing a positive or negative attitude toward that topic. Hence if A is influenced negatively by a blog B (A links to B, or comments on B, to show how B is wrong about a particular topic), then from the marketing/PR point of view influencing B in one direction will not be of much use if the aim is to influence A in the same direction. Opinions can also be manifested as biases. If a particular blogging community has grown up around an enthusiasm for some activity or product, then identifying and influencing opinion leaders on the topic that has already enthused the community is unlikely to be of much benefit. Kale et al. [179] use these ideas of link polarity and trust propagation (see Section 5.4) to discover like-minded blogs and try to extend the technique for more general purposes like discovering trustworthy nodes in Web graphs. When one blog links to another, the link polarity can be discovered via sentiment analysis of the text surrounding the link.

Recent work on microblogging [167] has shown that despite the smallness of the communications, people do use Twitter to gather information. Indeed, that is the primary use of Twitter when tweets that contain brand names are analysed; Jansen et al. found that over 80% of tweets containing brand names also contained no linguistic terms associated with positive or negative evaluation (i.e., the tweets expressed no opinion, and instead were searches for or sharing information). Of those in which opinions were expressed, about 50% of the tweets were clearly positive, while about 33% were clearly negative. Jansen et al.'s analysis confirms the finding that word of mouth tends to be U-shaped — that is that people are very keen to communicate and share very good or very bad experiences.

Nevertheless, we must also be aware that achieving something online — trending on Twitter — is not the same as achieving something offline — such as selling more widgets or winning an election. Mitchell and Hitlin [249] have shown that in the US, reaction on Twitter about major political events is very often at odds with traditional polling. It is sometimes more liberal than the survey results, and sometimes more conservative, but the most striking difference was the greater negativity on the microblogging site. The overall political reach of Twitter is relatively modest, with 13% of American adults using Twitter and just 3% regularly tweeting or retweeting news headlines [292]. Twitter users are also unrepresentative of the American public, being generally younger and more inclined to the Democratic Party [111]. More to the point, it is not always (and maybe rarely) the case that offline actors are active online. There may be many minority groups or identities who are marginalised, or end up on the wrong side of a digital divide, who simply do not have a prominent enough Web presence to appear as a statistically significant term during automated data crunching [70, 163, 266]. This analysis squares with that of Jansen et al. [167], in that the disparity reported by Mitchell and Hitlin [249] appears to stem from the large number of partisan tweets by committed Republicans and Democrats who are disproportionately either happy or mad-as-hell with certain people, events or news items.

Given these considerations, it seems that there is an effect of opinion on the likelihood of influence. Java et al. [169] have used topic analysis in their system *Feeds That Matter*, one of whose applications is to discover influential blogs in particular topic spaces. They imagine a user subscribing to a few blogs on a topic and wishing to read other influence leaders or opinion formers in the area. They assume that a link from A to B means that A has been influenced by B. Their ILIP algorithm (Identifying Leaders using Influence Propagation) uses this influence graph to determine influence leaders using the blogs already subscribed to as a seed set. The seed blogs induce a set of followers (blogs often influenced by members of the seed set). A linear threshold influence propagation model iterated over the whole graph will pull out topical influential nodes. This works broadly speaking by (a) looking at the number of links from A to B as a proportion of the number of links from A, and (b) if the total number of links to B or its neighbours exceeds a certain threshold, inferring influence [140, 170].

Mutz [260] notes that a great deal of research has shown that in political networks, wide-ranging debate has two perhaps surprising effects. First, exposure to and argument with opposing views tends to make people more tolerant of opposite points of view, which at least in the political realm would generally be considered a good thing. However secondly, it turns out that such exposure also reduces political participation, so the loss of fervour leads not only to tolerance but also lack of commitment. This means, for instance, that challenging ideas can win readers over, yet by diluting their commitment to their own point of view, it makes them less inclined to participate. In the sphere of politics, this connects with the unfortunate fact that commitment to the common good is a notoriously bad motivator.

On the other hand, McClurg [236] argues that this explanation is not sufficient to explain all the observed phenomena in such networks. For instance, another factor of importance is the amount of expertise in a network: "knowledgeable political discussants provide access to information that helps people recognize and reject dissonant political views, develop confidence in their attitudes, and avoid attitudinal ambivalence, thereby making participation more likely." In other words, people in such networks become more political, and begin to include political affiliation in their identity. Hence, to increase participation in a network, and in the activities around which a network is structured, it is very important for the network expertise/credibility hierarchy to be not too shallow (i.e., for it to be more complex than a few well-connected nodes and many others), and for there to be lots of argument and discussion, implying a rich stock of amplifiers, curators and commentators. It has also been noted, with respect to Islamic extremism, that the quality of their networks is a key determining factor among Muslim clerics as to whether they strategically adopt or reject Jihadi ideology. Analysis of tens of thousands of fatwas, articles and books reveals that career incentives depending on clerical educational networks are extremely important. Well-connected clerics are able to pursue comfortable careers within state-run religious institutions, rejecting Jihadi ideology in exchange for continued material support from the state. Meanwhile, clerics with poor educational networks, without the connections to help them advance, circumvent the state-run system by appealing directly to lay audiences for support. Jihadi ideology helps these badly-networked clerics by demonstrating to potential supporters costly commitment and unwillingness to compromise with political elites [264]. Hence it may be that the depth of expertise in a network discussed in Ref. [236] should also be linked to the connections of that network to effective political structures.

5.3 Measuring Influence

Influence is an important commodity on today's commercial Web. The amount of data that Web traffic generates has enabled a new range of business models (for instance, Google's business model is based on advertising, revolutionised beyond traditional mass media techniques by the precision with which Google can determine who clicked on what, when). Microblogging sites and SNSs provide forums where messages are spread, and where their reception can be measured and sometimes quantified. In this subsection, we will briefly survey what metrics are becoming available.

5.3.1 Measuring Influence Quantitatively

The idea of analysing networks of bloggers to determine influence has been explored in various ways. An early idea was to examine the network topology to discover central nodes. Centrality could be defined in a number of ways. *Degree* centrality is discovered via the number of relationships a node has, so the central nodes will be the most highly connected ones. *Closeness* centrality is discovered by examining the shortest paths between all the nodes; summing these will give a closeness metric. *Betweenness* centrality measures the number of times a node is on the shortest path between other pairs of nodes, so the most central nodes in this respect are vital links between nodes. Calvó-Armengol et al. [78] argue that "one (and only one) of such network measures captures exactly how each agent subsumes at equilibrium the network peer influence," referring to a specific type of measure of network centrality that counts, for each node, the total number of direct and indirect paths of any length in the network from that node, weighted with a factor that decays with path length. Karpf [181] adds other ideas to centrality, including link density, site traffic and community activity to create an overall measure of the importance of political blogs.

However, these topographic notions are not adequate for understanding the content dynamics of networks such as the blogosphere — they have very little connection with *content* at all. Clearly an idea starter might be very influential but poorly connected. Similarly, a reader may be very promiscuous and therefore very connected, but not influential at all. Therefore the next steps considered by the research community were to quantify influence by trying to understand different types of relationship between nodes in the network, and weighting them appropriately. Researchers began to measure ideas such as information diffusion, the extent to which information is spread across the network by links or trackback. The diffusion rate describes content dynamics in terms of the rate at which information is diffused around the network [328]. One measure of influence in economic networks is the *network value* of a customer, which is the expected profit to a supplier of goods obtained from other customers whose buying behaviour is influenced by that customer [107]. The notion of assimilation was defined: a content consumer is assimilated by content providers when his behaviour is influenced by theirs, and his characteristics become similar to theirs.

There are a number of models of measuring assimilation. The linear threshold model [140] posits a threshold for influence on a content consumer, and when the sum of influences exceeds that threshold, the consumer is regarded as having been assimilated. This therefore privileges network effects and word of mouth influence. The independent cascade model [137] uses probability to determine assimilation; what was the probability of similar behaviours being genuine influence, and in which direction? Kempe et al. [184] unified the two approaches, and showed that, on some basic assumptions, their model of the spread of influence provided an algorithm, also based on probability, that approached optimality (producing the optimal solution is NP-hard). There are important areas where this technique is applicable, but in a portion of a genuine blogosphere, the relevant probabilities will be extremely difficult to determine. Indeed, the only way to determine them for a given population may well be via post-hoc empirical investigation, sacrificing predictive power.

Hence these network-based approaches, through improvements on the straightforward analysis of network topology, are still inadequate to determine different roles in the diffusion of information. If influence is conceived as a graph, then the influence-tracking problem becomes the problem of predicting when and where new links will be created in the future. As Liben-Nowell and Kleinberg [217] argue, a surprising amount of information can be deduced from the analysis of the basic structure of a social network for link prediction. However, even the best of the predictors they survey is not too effective (accurate 16% of the time). Despite the increase in complexity, these methods still posit too flat a nexus of influence, and do not distinguish between different types of behaviour; in their discussion section Liben-Nowell and Kleinberg speculate on what extra information could improve the figure of 16%.

Studies of microblogging began with an advantage with respect to network analysis because of the simple structures the medium affords, meaning that the spread of influence was relatively straightforward to measure — how often is one retweeted? The range of easily detectable behaviours was also relatively small; how often does a user tweet? How often is he retweeted? How often does he retweet? How many followers? However, building on these early methods, Twitter analysis has become very much more complex, and new methods for measuring and comparison are appearing all the time [72, 73].

For example, Gaffney [128] discovered in his study of the Twittersphere in the context of the disputed Iranian election that influence, as measured by the numbers of retweets, varied over time, which meant that the data capture needed to contain the temporal dimension. He had to develop sub-network graphs of day-by-day, hour-by-hour and minute-by-minute data in order to discover the dynamic patterns of influence. But these analyses remain controversial — Morozov [256] argues that such structures fail to capture the deeper relationships and drivers, often leading to false ideas of what is actually going on in disputed events.

Backstrom et al. [23], studying the behaviour of people deciding to join groups, found that the number of people within the group to which potential joiners were already connected was important, as was the connectivity between those friends already within the group. People tend to want to join groups where there is already a rich support network in place, rather than groups in which there are lots of unrelated friends all of whom independently and for different reasons are enticing them to join. This latter finding implies that trust is a more important causal factor than information-finding; the unrelated friends structure is likely to be more efficient for information finding.

The paper is a very rich set of analyses and interpretations of group membership behaviour, and repays study. However, its method of using very large numbers and patterns (one experiment looked at 17m examples of the behaviour of non-members of groups who had friends within the group) means that the more basic drivers and patterns of influence are necessarily neglected. Once more, threshold models predominated; the analysis was well-tuned to detecting the cumulative effect of a number of sources of potential influence, and what the relationships between those influences may be (i.e., whether they would be more effective if they were themselves connected). Yet the analysis did not attempt to distinguish other types of remote influence — for instance, how often do people join groups because someone with whom they are unconnected, but whom they admire, is a member? The authors discussed the possibility, not yet realised, of connecting theoretical models of diffusion in social networks with their own network analyses. The data they had was very rich, but even so they found it challenging to formulate useful research questions. The work reported is impressive in extracting information from this data, but nevertheless remains hard to interpret in the micro-causal terms with which we are familiar in the description of behaviour.

In the blogosphere or Twittersphere, a user is influenced by a piece of information or article which may be mediated by other users. How can we understand the importance of the mediating users, and how this affects the content dynamics of the influential information? The results

of Szabo and Huberman [338] show that in popular Web 2.0 sites Digg
and YouTube, early effects of influence via social networks are quickly
dwarfed by the ease of finding very popular items. Once something has
appeared on the front page of Digg, then the social networking effect
is minor in comparison. Leskovec et al. discovered in their studies of
recommender systems that the purchases of recommended items tend
to be a very small proportion of purchases as a whole. They were able
to categorise the interactions on the basis of network properties —
number of nodes in the network, number of edges, number of recommenders, number of receivers of recommendations, number of recommendations, price of the product, number of reviews, average product
rating. Their regression model suggested some characteristics of products and communities in which recommendations had a better chance
of being taken up:

> ... we find that the numbers of nodes and receivers have
> negative coefficients, showing that successfully recom-
> mended products are actually more likely to be not so
> widely popular. The only attributes with positive coef-
> ficients are the number of recommendations r, number
> of edges e, and price p. This shows that more expensive
> and more recommended products have a higher success
> rate. These recommendations should occur between a
> small number of senders and receivers, which suggests
> a very dense recommendation network where lots of
> recommendations are exchanged between a small com-
> munity of people. These insights could be of use to
> marketers — personal recommendations are most effec-
> tive in small, densely connected communities enjoying
> expensive products [206].

One important issue in measuring influence is the problem — hard
to solve without a deeper analysis — of distinguishing between *influence*, where A's behaviour causes B to behave in a similar way, *correlation*, where A and B are similar types and behave in similar ways
without actually influencing each other at all, and *external influence*,
when environmental factors induce A and B to behave in similar ways.

There are some methods to attempt to deal with this — for instance, Anagnostopoulos et al. [13] propose a shuffle test, which analyses both the real actions and also the same actions with shuffled time stamps, on the general theory that shuffling time stamps will affect correlation when influence is genuine, but should show the same amount of correlation if it is down to accidental similarities between A and B (Szabo and Huberman [338] use a similar method to test correlation and causation). The shuffle test showed some value in experiments, but was not able to go beyond a qualitative measure of the existence of influence, rather than a quantitative measure of its strength, or a classification of its type.

The correlation problem remains serious for automated network analysis. This may be partly thanks to problematic feedback effects, where the similarity between two individuals and the influence they have on each other increasing in tandem together [95], and partly because influence is modelled so crudely in networks. The latter is evidence of a trade-off; the more complex and larger the networks analysed, the less fine-grained the representations will have to be in order to prevent combinatorial explosion. Hence this kind of analysis will be less suitable to the discovery of particularly efficient kinds of influence. Indeed, Crandall et al. [95] argue that macro-scale analysis of networks can profitably be augmented by examining specific behaviour in terms of its content and context. Quantitative and qualitative study go hand in hand.

5.3.2   Measuring Influence Qualitatively

Qualitative social scientists have also studied Web 2.0 developments, both for their own sake and for their potential for promoting learning. Such work is often ideologically committed to the ideas of egalitarianism, participation, communication and empowerment, and hence tends not to focus on unearthing hierarchies of influence; indeed, they often see the role of Web 2.0 normatively as dismantling hierarchies and distributing influence more widely. One route for this sort of work to go is to uncover the formal codes and norms that govern Web 2.0 interaction, to enable its use in structured learning environments. As Lewis et al.

put it, "The formal structures inscribed in code become manifested in social actions that further inscribe patterned social categories." [214] Or, in terms familiar from the work of Bourdieu [65], the habitus generated by the allowed forms of interaction (commenting, rating, trackback, etc.) generates a doxa, or a way of thinking about interaction in that space which makes it seem natural and common sense.

The more radical qualitative social scientists are keener on disrupting this doxa to increase the visibility of alternative methods of interaction, than in mapping the current position. This may backfire in the short term; some social scientists have discovered that blogging and Tweeting have sufficient credibility to have become important public spaces for debate. In the last few decades, the mass media, with their high barriers to entry, have played this role almost exclusively, which means that 'ordinary' people have great difficulty in finding a voice and achieving public acceptance of 'their' problems. Maratea has found that bloggers can bypass the mass media bottleneck, and air their problems in such a way as to engage public opinion — although ultimately, credibility rests in all but a few cases on issues being eventually taken up by the traditional media. His analysis does not question the hierarchy of blogs with a few highly-read, highly-connected and highly-linked-to blogs at the top, and many others with negligible readership. The factors that he finds important in getting a narrative taken seriously (based on studies of the blogosphere and also standard media) are drama, novelty, saturation and topics that resonate culturally [231].

The motivations of content providers do not remain constant. In particular, many bloggers begin by using their blog as a means of expression, and only after some time do they begin to try to extend their influence. So, for example, in one survey based on self-reports of American political bloggers [117], the top three reasons that respondents claimed moved them to begin blogging were: 'to let off steam', 'to keep track of [their] thoughts', and 'to formulate new ideas'. Each of these motivations, we note, is entirely selfish though not commercial, and imply that the bloggers were interested primarily in developing their own thoughts and communicating them to the world. However, the top three reasons bloggers gave for *continuing* their blogs were: 'to provide an alternative perspective to the mainstream media', 'to inform people about the most relevant information on topics of interest', and 'to influence public opinion.' It seems plausible that bloggers aim to be idea starters at an early stage in their careers, but, at least in politics, graduate to communicating ideas, knowledge and debate to wide audiences, which implies that they shift their self-image and increasing their influence becomes their key motivational factor.

Another hard-to-quantify factor in influence is the perception of the personal characteristics of the content provider. Relevance emerges in terms of both perceived identity and constructed identity. Aral and Walker [18], Armstrong and McAdams [19] and Trammell and Keshelashvili [349] have found that gender is an important determiner of perceived credibility — for example, blogs written by those whose profiles identify them as men are generally deemed more credible by both men and women. Armstrong and McAdams place this result in the context of information-seeking; it is a reasonably robust result across a number of media that information or expertise is seen as more credible when gathered from men, and the blogs that they used for their experiments were particularly ones intended to function as information sources. On the other hand, the distancing nature of the medium may also play a part — genderless blogs did not lack credibility. Trammell and Keshelashvili [349] discovered that some gender-stereotypical behaviour continues online. Women tend to self-disclose more and adopt a diary style, while men disclose less and present information, while as readers women are interested in communication and men in information gathering. Aral and Walker's [18] large-scale study of Facebook showed that men were more influential than women when trying to get people to adopt a particular product, and that women tend not to be influenced by other women (women were much more influential on men than women). There are also age differences: in perception of blogs, young people seem to prefer a more informal style, and find blogs more credible in general, while in the Facebook study, younger users were more susceptible to influence than older users [18].

For the individual, particularly young people, identity is bound up with interactions with the network, and feedback is an important measure of worth — hence influence is certainly sought. For young people, "that they have something that gets circulated indicates to them not so much that they posted something worthy of attention as much as their own social status and their centrality to the community. A quality post may or may not get feedback, but a popular person surely will" [214]. This ties in with the fact that in many SNSs people interact with people they know, or who live geographically close to them; the virtuality of many social networks is less than one might expect [252]. It also ties in with the general rule in social psychology that 'birds of a feather flock together.' Li and Chignell [216] produced experimental evidence to show that blog readers were significantly more likely to be attracted to (and presumably therefore influenced by, although Li and Chignell did not specifically test for this) blogs written by bloggers of similar personality. Readers were, they showed, able to judge personality characteristics from the small amount of usually linguistic evidence on show in the blog (both bloggers and readers in this small-scale experiment self-rated their own personalities).

Those bloggers who have well-known offline personalities to leverage (celebrities, politicians, journalists, etc.) seem to have greater influence, all things being equal, yet are more cautious about the ideas they spread. Highly popular bloggers are very concerned with self-presentation [349]. A study of blogs of UK politicians showed that they were not interested in driving debates.

> On occasion, our parliamentarians posted entries that were unique to their blog; on others, they repackaged questions asked in Parliament or contributions made in seminars. Some posts were journal-like in content and tone, whilst others resembled an administrative note in a constituency newsletter [124].

The most influential blog in this particular sample was that of Boris Johnson, but even he used his blog as a means of self-promotion and a complement to his offline personality, rather than to spread any ideas *per se*. He is now the Mayor of London. But in this as in many things, he is an outlier; in general the Parliamentarians in the survey were keener to avoid risk than make a splash.

5.4　Trust Propagation and Recommendation

Trust is an important factor in influence [23, 136, 179]. Graph theory provides means to model trust and recommendation. Trust propagation refers to the spread of trust through a network (we can model trust in a directed graph with a directed edge between two nodes from the trustor to the trustee) based on assumed transitivity or partial transitivity (i.e., if A trusts B and B trusts C, A may, in some circumstances, come to trust C because of confidence in B's judgment). Trust propagation is of practical use in recommendation, so that if C is judged by a recommender system to be 'close enough' to A in the relevant tastes and respects, then items that C has enjoyed may confidently be recommended to A. Recommendation and trust interact, so that the former may help foster the latter; if A has enjoyed sufficiently many of a system's recommendations, he may come to trust the output of the recommendation algorithm, and so to that extent could be said to have fostered trust in the judgments of the anonymous agents who are the subjects of the data input to the algorithm. This indeed is what might be expected, given the emphasis in Ref. [291] on the role of social networks in supporting trust in recommender systems; recommendations do not take place in a vacuum, but already assume a possibly informal network of users in a social context with some trust relations already in place. Recommendation systems can therefore be seen as a special case of social networks which make and foster connections between people. Recommendation is irreducibly social, and connections are made on the back of explicit user models or indirectly through the revelation of existing implicit connections between people through crunching data. Mathematically, Andersen et al. [14] have argued that a trust network has a complex structure, and an intuitive set of axioms cannot be jointly satisfied.

One sometimes overlooked dimension is that of trust versus distrust. In their studies of recommendation systems, Victor et al. [358] argue that performance can be improved if ratings of *distrust* are factored in, alongside trust ratings for recommenders. In particular, they cite the issue of controversial reviews, which receive enthusiastic approval from a large number of readers, and scathing disapproval from many others. This makes an interesting intuitive point. A new idea is likely to be controversial. It will be uncontextualised. Its ramifications will not be clear immediately. Most of its important implications will be in the minds of the readers, and will therefore reflect their interests. Neither enthusiasts nor detractors will immediately find evidence conflicting with their initial judgment. It seems to follow that the products of an original thinker will tend to be rated at the extremes (good and bad), and that we might expect less enthusiasm, both positive and negative, and less controversy, surrounding those who mediate ideas rather than originate them.

Leskovec et al. [209] have investigated the patterns of trust and distrust in Wikipedia promotions to try to provide insights into the applicability of certain older social theories to SNSs, specifically structural balance theory [81, 154, 155], which postulates that both a friend of a friend, and an enemy of an enemy, are friends (and conversely enemies of friends are enemies), and status theory, which trades on the insights that a positive link may indicate not only trust, but also a recognition from the linker that the linkee has a higher status (and conversely, a negative link may be a recognition of lower status), and that such judgments may percolate transitively through the network [144]. These two theories make different predictions, even on simple triads where we try to predict the relationship between A and B given that we know about A's and B's relationships to a third party C. Furthermore, structural balance theory produces undirected graphs, while the graphs in status theory are directed. Leskovec et al. [209] found that the data in a number of datasets favoured the status theory, but that structural balance theory was also confirmed in some respects and contexts. The datasets they looked at were surprisingly uniform in structure, so that rules learned from, say, Wikipedia applied reasonably well to Epinions [208]. One interesting wrinkle was the unexpected discovery that people have harsher opinions about people of roughly equivalent status to themselves [207], although whether that is caused by the pressures of competition or by a greater critical understanding of such people's performance must be a matter for further experiment and investigation.

Network and graph theory provide important entry points into understanding how particular structures feed back into individual behaviour. However, it should also be pointed out that there are alternative ways of conceiving the network and the role of the individual nodes in transmitting information and attitudes. Yeaman et al. [380] have investigated the persistence (and even the spread) of misinformation within communities which nevertheless have a propensity to eliminate ideas with low intrinsic value. They develop the construct of a *cultural load* of misinformation which can be maintained within a culture despite its low value. The spread of the cultural load is not correlated with architectural constructs, such as the individual's degree of connection or the rate at which information is eliminated. Rather, the relative rates at which individuals transmit or eliminate traits have a stronger impact, implying that "changes in communications technology may have influenced cultural evolution more strongly through changes in the amount of information flow, rather than the details of who is connected to whom". The affordances of technology are more influential, on this model, than the local knowledge or connections of the individuals in the network. It is not who you know, but how easily you can communicate.

6

Control: The Exogenous Global

This is an art
Which does mend nature — change it rather — but
The art itself is nature.

The Winter's Tale, act IV scene iv

The Web, unlike many other complex systems, does not have a *telos* or function. That impedes attempts to develop mechanisms as methods of indirect control, as neuroscientist Steven Pinker argued (in relation to the Internet, although the argument applies to the Web *mutatis mutandis*).

> The Internet is in some ways like a brain, but in important ways not. The brain doesn't just let information ricochet around the skull. It is organized to *do* something: to move the muscles in ways that allow the whole body to attain the goals set by the emotions. The anatomy of the brain reflects that: it is not a uniform web or net, but has a specific organization in which emotional circuits interconnect with the frontal lobes, which receive information from perceptual systems and

send commands to the motor system. This goal-directed
organization comes from an important property of
organisms ...: their cells are in the same reproductive
boat, and thus have no "incentive" to act against the
interests of the whole body. But the Internet, not being
a cohesive replicating system, has no such organization,
and, I would think, no goal or direction [294].

Having made this point, it is also worth noting conversely that the
Web needs to preserve certain properties or *invariants* to allow information to flow efficiently and for it to serve the diverse purposes of its
millions or even billions of users [44]. This sort of analysis has been
done for the Internet both by engineers and those in Internet studies.
For instance, Liu et al. [221] set out an analysis of the needs of the
future generation Internet to assess whether it should be developed in
an evolutionary manner from the current infrastructure, or whether
an entirely new architecture should be defined. They identify seven
features that the future Internet should possess, including scalability,
security and an equitable economic structure, while noting four important contradictions which exacerbate the complexity of the development task: (i) between the complex diversity of network functions and
the single-dimension scalability of the architecture, (ii) between the
fixed transmission and control goals of the network and its unknown
and unpredictable behaviour, (iii) between the security and trustworthiness requirements of the network and its inherent vulnerability, and
(iv) between the variability of network needs and the stability of the
architecture [221].

Meanwhile, a few commentators such as Mansell and Steinmuller
[230] have analysed the Internet in terms of what policymakers or crit-
ics wish it to achieve, and have commented on the relative lack of depth
of the evidence base for evaluating policy, and the (in)ability of governments, infrastructure companies and software companies to 'drive' the
Internet in a particular direction [230]. However, there are relatively
few comparable analyses for the Web.

In the final section of our monograph, we will discuss some methods of trying to produce specific desired behaviours in the Web. As

noted in Section 2.3, such a survey can only scratch the surface. However, as described in that section, and shown in Figure 2.1, the work we describe here will hopefully cover the interactions between the Web and both individuals and society, and also the contribution that mathematics/science and engineering/technology can make. In Section 6.1, we cover some general issues to do with control in emergent systems, and illustrate these in the context of the Web with examples from analysis (looking at how discrete mathematics can help identify vulnerabilities, Section 6.1.1) and engineering (looking at how Web Science can be seen as an example of reflective practice, Section 6.1.2). Section 6.2 considers various aspects of the attempt to move from a Web of linked documents to a Web of linked data. Section 6.3 considers the two-way interactions between the Web and the world of politics. Section 6.4 looks at how the data needs of individuals are determining new structures and architectures. Finally, Section 6.5 returns in more detail to the idea of a social machine to enable communities and groups to use the power of networks and data to achieve their social ends.

6.1 Control in Emergent Systems

The emergent phenomena we have discussed in Sections 3–5 have been genuinely emergent — actors acting for a specific reason, and phenomena which (if they had been designed at all) were designed for a specific and local purpose, interacting at scale to produce unintended (though not necessarily bad) macro-level consequences. The engineering goal of Web Science as argued in the earliest papers [44, 45] was to ensure that the Web had positive social benefits, but the preceding discussions in this monograph show how complex are the relations between the micro and the macro in order to make this happen. Code, norms and regulations constrain what individuals can do, but equally structuration theory reminds us that they do have agency within those constraints, and their decisions will in turn affect the structures that constrain them.

Furthermore, the whole notion of 'control' of the Web is controversial — commentators such as Morozov have complained about what has been called 'solutionism', which imputes to the Web (and the Internet more generally) a broader logic, and which allows the Web to be mis-described as a technical solution or fix for every problem. In the worst types of solutionism, states of society that happen to run against this presumed logic of technological development can get reframed as 'problems' to be 'solved' by more technology [257].

It is worth remembering in this context that according to some commentators on emergence, ignorance is useful. For instance, in the context of the organisation of ant colonies,

> The simplicity of the ant language — and the relative stupidity of the individual ants — is, as the computer programmers say, a feature not a bug. Emergent systems can grow unwieldy when their component parts become excessively complicated. Better to build a densely interconnected system with simple elements, and let the more sophisticated behavior trickle up. (That's one reason why computer chips traffic in the streamlined language of zeros and ones.) Having individual agents capable of directly assessing the overall state of the system can be a real liability in swarm logic, for the same reason that you don't want one of the neurons in your brain to suddenly become sentient [173, p. 78].

This outlines the difficulty of the engineering challenge — it is essential not to put the desired functionality into the individuals in the network (the mistake of trying to design intelligent ants). The challenge is to create an environment in which relatively simple elements combine to create a harmonious whole.

6.1.1   From Analysis to Engineering

Yet engineering and policy goals remain important — the whole success of the Web depends on its positive social benefits. No doubt any benefits can be only partial and temporary, and prone to being undermined or gamed by malefactors (or just by the unintended consequences of people repurposing technology and creating something new and surprising).

Nevertheless, the discoveries made by research methods covered in the previous three sections may drive more constructive thinking. For instance, Zhang et al. [386] uses network science techniques to study the dynamics of consensus formation and social influence, and has developed models to argue that a committed minority of about 10% of a population can convert most others to their way of thinking. Data from Facebook and Twitter can be used to evaluate and adjust the model.

This sort of empirically validated account of influence (we surveyed several other examples in Sections 5.2 and 5.3) could be the first stage of delivering an understanding of how to drive such consensus-formation. As one example of such ambition, the FuturICT project (http://www.futurict.eu/) aims to put such models into practice by understanding and managing complex, global and socially-interactive systems.

As a larger example of the practical value of scientific understanding of the Web, let us consider work taking the perspective of the Web as an information network as a means to identify and minimise vulnerabilities. Network analysis allows consideration of how robust a network can be, and how vulnerable to attack. Scale-free networks are quite robust against decay as most nodes have relatively minor degree, and therefore there are very few whose disappearance could disrupt the connectivity of the network in a catastrophic way. The critical point at which the network will fall apart would only occur after the disappearance of a very large number of nodes indeed, and if the network continued to grow it would retain its integrity thanks to the presence of the hubs [10]. On the other hand, this tells us something about the Web's vulnerabilities — a deliberate strategy of attacking the hubs will damage a scale-free network disproportionately. Hence the hubs need extra protection. We should also note in passing the paradox of control; the same analyses that enable the Web's benefits to be noted and protected can also provide valuable information to malefactors.

Graphs and networks are also valuable in understanding and minimising the spread of epidemics. If a node's susceptibility to a virus- or worm-spread epidemic is proportional to the number of infected neighbours, then mathematical parameters can be developed to express the likelihood of an epidemic spreading [233]. With a finite bounded-degree graph (i.e., there are no hubs or authorities beyond a certain size), the infection will die out eventually, the issue being whether it does so in polynomial (i.e., short) or exponential (too long) time; the relevant parameter here is a function of the likelihood of infection. For a preferential attachment graph with well-connected hubs such as the Web, this parameter value for the polynomial outcome is 0 — i.e., any infection will almost certainly take exponential time to die out [39, 287]. Hence even viruses with a very small rate of spread have a good chance of becoming epidemic. Digital communications can then be used to confirm these models; for instance, Dong et al. [108] use empirical data from smartphones within small communities to understand the networks of communication that facilitate the spread of epidemics.

The mathematics of graphs enables scientists to determine good strategies for halting epidemics. With a preferential attachment graph with bounded *average* degree, it has been shown that the strategy of targeting those nodes with a large number of neighbours will wipe out the epidemic quickly and without large expenditure of resources. In particular, if an 'antidote' is distributed proportionately to the number of neighbours, then an epidemic will be contained [59].

6.1.2   Web Engineering as Reflective Practice

Control in the Web context is made even more difficult not simply by the emergent nature of the phenomena to be controlled or influenced, but also because of the scale involved. The Web is unusually large, complex and decentralised. Because of the *sui generis* nature of socially embedded engineering problems on this scale much of the relevant knowledge, which is typically procedural rather than declarative, must be derived in practice, often in response to unforeseen challenges perceived during a project itself. This has led to the development of a theory of engineering practice called *reflective practice* [273, 311].

In this methodology, the problem as initially set is not fixed in stone, as the practitioner must change her perceptions and strategy in response to uncertainty, instability and unique features of a problem. She proceeds experimentally, but not, as in the scientific context, using the logic of confirmation; rather the logic is of affirmation. The aim is not to raise hypotheses to falsify them (as with Popper's falsification logic of scientific discovery — [295]) but to create and discover new solutions that need to be neither unique nor optimal. Controlled experiments are out of the question because their effects cannot be restricted or reversed, and so each experiment that the engineer tries must as far as possible be sensitive to the needs of the context. The systems knowledge cannot be tested in isolation.

The relation between change and understanding is different in reflective practice precisely because of the impracticality of controlled experiments. The imperative to understand is subservient to the requirement to change for the better (unlike in disinterested research, where understanding is an autonomous goal). The ever-present danger is that an experiment makes a permanent change for the worse.

An extra and unusual issue is the variance of scale between the experimental setup and the outcome. Any experimental change will be of relatively small scale — a new type of software, a new type of communications protocol. The consequences *relative to the intention of the innovation* can be described and studied in small-scale experiments in the lab, or with a small set of pioneer users. Such intentions are usually focused on the experience of a single user or a single organisation. The problem, of course, is that few if any of the massive global consequences of Web technologies are of this tractable type, because they affect very large groups of people and organisations, so that even the benign or positive consequences at the scale of the Web as a whole are unintended.

Engineering using reflective practice inevitably involves trade-offs between the impact of an artefact in relation to its intention, and the full set of consequences both intended and unintended [311, p. 153ff.], but the Web is an especially difficult case because the impacts in relation to the intention of the engineered development are relatively small-scale and detectable fairly quickly, while the unintended consequences, good and bad, emerge years later at a scale far beyond the control of a single person or corporation.

One way of expressing this mismatch is to look at three levels of analysis in the evaluation of design. First, the design specification includes a normative element against which it can be evaluated ("the artefact should do X"). Second, any design detail has to be evaluated against and be consistent with previous design decisions. Third, the designer must be sensitive to any new problems that arrive during deployment. The third level brings in phenomena at the macro-scale which may take years to manifest themselves. So distributed and decentralised is the Web that even the second level is likely to be beyond the individual design team's capacity for understanding.

Another illuminating way of looking at the problem is through the lens of the transdisciplinarity framework [145], which postulates three kinds of knowledge, of systems, targets and transformations. The Web engineer is possessed of the systems knowledge of the artefact being constructed, while the target knowledge describes the interests of the major stakeholders. Hence the systems and target knowledge are, from the point of view of the individual engineering project, tractable. However, the transformation knowledge, of all the various systems relevant to implementation and use, is key, and yet is once more out of reach of the immediate designer. It describes the macro-level problems that need to be addressed — problems which are caused precisely when the system's use and significance extends beyond the intended stakeholder group.

Each of these tripartite frameworks implies that engineering large-scale Web phenomena is a painstaking process which ideally will seek consensus and will provide a range of people with solutions to genuine issues, or with transformative opportunities. Guaranteeing this is non-trivial, of course, but in the rest of this final section we will consider some long-term projects which highlight the scale and ambition of the control issue and show what can be achieved.

6.2   The Linked Data Web

Data is often marked by clear structure and semantics, yet the traditional Web of documents does not contain the machinery to exploit these to the full. Data appears in shapeless dumps, in formats such as CSV which do not express its structure, in proprietary formats which hinder reuse, and even formats which remove all structure, such as pdf.

The challenge of creating the Linked Data Web (LDW) is to try to reap the benefits of a world where data is directly linked with other relevant data in machine-accessible ways, by using open standards and universally valid identifiers. The formalisms are available, such as the knowledge representation language RDF, which uses URIs to identify objects and relations [42, 229]. Much of the technology is already in place [151, 152], while the Semantic Web has already been discussed in a Web Science context [44, 317, pp. 17–39]. Browsers, search engines and query languages are appearing, and the technology requirements for navigating an unbounded global data space and opening it out to end users as well as programmers and developers are beginning to be understood [46, 180].

The Linking Open Data project has been monitoring the development of the LDW since 2007 [51], and by 2012 was estimating its size to be about 52 billion RDF triples, as noted in Section 1.1. DBpedia (http://dbpedia.org/About) was the first major effort to publish linked data [21], but now contributions are coming increasingly from companies, governments and other public sector bodies such as libraries, statistical bodies or environmental agencies. In parallel, Google, Yahoo! and Bing have established the schema.org initiative, a shared set of schemata for publishing structured data on the Web that focuses on vocabulary agreement and low barriers of entry for data publishers (http://schema.org/).

Once data is placed in a file using W3C standards, it can be processed, for example putting it in a spreadsheet, or (if it has a geolocation) on a map. It can also be linked in two ways. First if the data was about a particular object X, it could be linked with other data about X. Second, the properties that the data expresses can be linked to the same properties in other data; for instance, if the data gives the population of Copenhagen, we can specify that by 'population' is meant what it means in DBpedia, or that 'Copenhagen' refers to the geographical entity defined in Danish law, and not the popular song of the 1920s recorded by Bix Beiderbecke and the Wolverine Orchestra. The links are made by using URIs across the datasets. By following the links made in this way, the LDW allows the user to gather large quantities of data about related things, or about related concepts. Berners-Lee

[42] sets out four guidelines for linking data. First, use URIs to name things, providing a uniform standard of naming. Second, use HTTP URIs, which allows others to look up the names and get access to resources (called *dereferencing* the URIs). Third, provide useful information for those who look up a URI, exploiting standards such as RDF, RDFS [68] and SPARQL [297, 345]. This information may be human-readable (in HTML), or machine-readable. Fourth, link to other URIs, in order to allow users to find other relevant datasets via the link structure of the LDW. Heath and Bizer [151] go into detail on the technical mechanics of this process.

6.2.1   Identity on the LDW

URIs are central to the LDW vision, but if they are understood as names, they inherit many of the practical and philosophical problems associated with naming. How do we establish that two instances of the same name refer to the same person? How do we reliably and scalably find all the names of a particular individual? This is a massive problem in the linked data world, even on the relatively small scale of current practice, simply because the LDW is a decentralised set of sets of fragments whose links may conflict with each other, and whose referents cannot be enumerated [133]. Anyone can create a URI to identify anything — a person, an abstract concept or an object you could drop on your foot — and state its equivalence to something else. Yet identity is a complex philosophical issue, and on the decentralised Web there is no central power to impose particular naming practices, or to limit the set of potential referents and the potential set of names. Hence the LDW is automatically going to be open to the same set of philosophical problems about identity as is natural language [377]. Indeed, it will often be worse because applications range over the entire Web, whereas in natural language there are often contextual limits to the range of potential referents — for instance, if two people refer to 'Paul Smith', they are almost certainly referring to a common acquaintance, and so there is no ambiguity even though there are millions of Paul Smiths across the globe. Identity is a classic Web Science issue, as it resists a purely technical solution while requiring technical understanding.

As noted, HTTP URIs are dereferenceable, allowing useful information (a description of the identified resource) to be returned when accessed, yet the question of what is identified remains complex (for example, how do we avoid confusing URIs for things with URIs for webpages for those things?). Glaser and Halpin [133] describe how HTTP 303 status codes allow redirects to get round such a problem, giving the following example.

> Thanks to little HTTP tricks called *303 redirection* and *content negotiation*, when a linked data application dereferences a linked data URI, that URI automatically redirects to another URI to return data in [RDF]. When accessed by a browser, the same URI redirects to yet another URI and returns a hypertext webpage with a human-readable description of the document. This hack creates three URIs from one: http://dbpedia.org/resource/Engelbert_Humperdinck for the thing itself, which then redirects to http:// dbpedia.org/data/Engelbert_Humperdinck for data, and http://dbpedia.org/html/Engelbert_Humperdinck for the webpage [133, p. 68].

Even so, however, there are still identity issues — there are, after all, two famous Engelbert Humperdincks (one the composer of *Hansel and Gretel* and the other the singer of *Please Release Me*) and maybe (though perhaps unlikely) a few non-famous ones.

The proliferation of URIs on the LDW depends on the practice of naming. Adding some data about Engelbert to the LDW requires a URI. This could be freshly minted, or it could be reused from another piece of data about EH. A URI could also be discovered via a number of routes. There are linked data/Semantic Web search engines such as Sindice (http://sindice.com/) which can retrieve other URIs (via keyword, so disambiguation may remain an issue). At the time of writing, Sindice returns about 3500 URIs for EH, some of which are obviously for the composer, some of which obviously for the singer, and others which are ambiguous at first sight). Existing datasets such as DBpedia or government open data sites also coin comprehensive and/or authoritative URIs.

Reuse of URIs helps with disambiguation if a name denotes other things; as noted above, if the data was about Copenhagen the city (as opposed to the football team or the interpretation of quantum mechanics or the song), then it could either be linked to, or use, the DBpedia URI for Copenhagen. Reuse is also valuable from the point of view of facilitating linking — the same URI refers to the same thing and so the link can easily be made. Yet the problem of reusing someone else's URI is that you don't have control — the resource in your dataset may be slightly different from the pre-existing one, or the original coiner of the URI may change its meaning [133].

It is in any case utopian to expect everyone in a decentralised world to use authoritative URIs. We should expect highly promiscuous coining of URIs, and try to negotiate a world where a resource will typically have many identifiers. There must be enough expressivity to allow equivalences to be asserted within applications, and to facilitate processing of many equivalent URIs as a group in such a world.

There is a sameAs relation in the Web Ontology Language OWL [100, 344], but its semantics are quite precise — to state that one thing is the owl:sameAs another is to assert that they are indiscernible, i.e., that they have the same properties. This is a very strong statement, and again begs a number of philosophical questions. In particular, identity is a metaphysical concept, whereas indiscriminability is epistemological. Both are reflexive and symmetric relations, but identity is transitive whereas indiscriminability is not [378]. Yet actually whether two things are effectively identical can often depend on the task at hand — two databases about Copenhagen the city may be comparable in some contexts, such as compiling a tourist guide, and yet differences in their interpretation of 'Copenhagen' might turn out to be critical for other purposes, such as estimating future demand for health services. Co-reference on this view is a type of knowledge — certainly a crucial type, but knowledge nonetheless — which may be dependent on context.

It is important to incorporate flexibility in an identity regime. As Glaser and Halpin [133] put it, "if a data producer finds it useful to consider two or more URIs equivalent, then asserting their equivalence is sensible; an application consuming this data, however, should check to make sure it trusts these relationships before mashing up properties or running an inference engine." Glaser et al. [134] describe the sameas.org service (http://sameas.org/), which takes a URI and then looks for URIs that may refer to the same thing, storing and publishing the list. The Simple Knowledge Organization System (SKOS), a W3C standard for representing knowledge organisation systems such as thesauri and taxonomies within the Semantic Web using RDF [166], contains properties such as exactMatch and closeMatch whose semantics are not as precise as terms in OWL, and which therefore do not make such a strong ontological commitment.

6.2.2 Consuming Data on the LDW

There has been a lot of attention focused on the formalisms and protocols for the LDW, and on tools such as linked data browsers, while the mushrooming linked data cloud has been a focus of interest. Yet one of the key factors in getting the LDW to work is the *consumption* of linked data. Publishing and linking data is certainly useful, but it needs to appear so that it is consumable by people using off-the-shelf systems whose main focus is utility and ease. Data should be easy to access and process. LDW engineers generally agree that ease of access is best served by RESTful APIs (based on Representational State Transfer — [125]), and ease of processing by the JavaScript Object Notation (JSON — [96], and http://www.json.org/), a lightweight, text-based, language-independent data interchange format.

One barrier to consumption is the up front effort of retrieval, storage and manipulation of the data by the consumer. However, as Heath [151] argues, it is unreasonable to expect that the benefits of the LDW will be trivial to achieve, given that data is gathered from a potentially wide range of distributed and heterogeneous sources. Data integration, even in closed environments as well as open ones, has always been a problematic concept, albeit one whose benefits outweigh its costs, and has been the subject of research for many years [106]. The LDW's competitive advantage stems from delivering the means to access data from distributed sources, with methods for discovery, merging and tracing [151]. Discovering data is a matter of following links (hence the plea for publishers to link data to other datasets — [42]). Meanwhile, certain places, such as DBpedia, are important hubs for the LDW; an important research focus is how to apply search engine queries to such sites [245]. Merging data is relatively straightforward because RDF is neutral between schemas and does not provide for validation. Hence RDF graphs can be merged easily without risking violating pre-existing schemas. Where two graphs contain the same URI, it is straightforward to combine them. Meanwhile, dereferencing a URI helps trace provenance. In this respect Heath [151] compares a data file in CSV, whose authenticity cannot easily be checked once it has left the publisher, with an equivalent set of linked data, whose URIs can always be dereferenced to check for anomalies or updates.

6.2.3   Ways Forward: From Engineering to Control

Given that it uses HTTP URIs as identifiers, HTTP as the retrieval mechanism and RDF to describe resources, the LDW sits on top of the W3C's architecture, and inherits many of its desirable properties. In particular, it is generic in terms of the data it can host; it is decentralised and open to anyone wishing to publish material; and there are no representational constraints in terms of the vocabularies used to express the data. The use of RDF links to connect entities creates a global data graph spanning data sources, facilitating their discovery [51].

The advantage of this approach is that the data is kept logically separate from formatting and presentational aspects. If an application comes across data described with an unfamiliar vocabulary, the URIs identifying vocabulary terms can be dereferenced to access definitions. The LDW allows completely open applications which access data sources on the fly, discovering new ones at runtime, rather than relying, as in the Web 2.0 mashup world, on data sources fixed in advance [51]. The use of the RDF data model simplifies data access in comparison to Web APIs, which use heterogeneous data models and thereby restrict access [46].

Publishing metadata alongside the data is important to facilitate trust and maximise utility. The metadata should cover the means of creating the data, as well as the date of creation (much data on the Web is perforce out of date) and information about its creator [148, 149, 150]. Vocabularies and data models for doing this have been developed as part of the Open Provenance Model [255], while Dezani-Ciancaglini et al. [103] introduce a calculus with operational semantics for expressing the provenance of linked data processing. Understanding provenance will help the LDW develop as a medium for scientific research; Moreau [254] argues that provenance information is crucial for allowing reproducibility of data creation, and the consequent validation of results both final and intermediate. This is one of the reasons why the Semantic Web has long been thought of as a key enabler for the development of e-science [104], and indeed as a means of administering it too [6]. In developing methods for assessing the trustworthiness of data, it is likely that different methods will be needed for particular 'brands' of data (e.g., from university departments, governments or respected private institutions), and then again for the 'long tail' of smaller data providers whose names are less well known (particularly if they work in a relatively unfamiliar domain). The complexities and requirements of expressing provenance information over an open and messy system such as the Web are reviewed in [253].

The development of the LDW is very much a Web Science issue, demanding technologies, protocols and practices that are self-sustaining and scalable, across a range of contexts, including e-science, government and the media. These processes reflect the descriptions of informationalism [82], in which knowledge acts upon knowledge as the main mode of production, and where knowledge about knowledge is a key commodity. The aim of the LDW is to use the principles of the Web to drill down beyond documents to the data itself. Hence human processing is taken out of the loop — a scientific paper is now often written via human synthesis of information from a series of documents created following a search for key terms, whereas under the LDW much of the effort to assemble the relevant data could be automated. As Castells [82, p. 17] writes, the orientation of informationalism is "toward the accumulation of knowledge and towards higher levels of complexity in information processing". The LDW seems to be a paradigm case of this kind of development, facilitating control of the massive linked knowledge structure that the Web now supports.

6.2.4   Open Data

In an initiative with relevance to the LDW, there has been a recent push toward publishing *open data* on the Web. Open data is characterised by three properties. First of all, it is machine-readable. Second, it is online. Third, it is available under an open licence. This last is extremely important — databases are usually protected with rules analogous to copyright, in order to protect the interests of database compilers. Copyright is the best instrument, because contracts are extremely difficult to enforce on an electronic database once it has been downloaded or accessed by a third party, (see [248] and [302] for discussions with a UK focus). With an open licence, the data owner allows unhindered, or virtually unhindered, irrevocable and royalty-free use of the data. Typical licence forms [198] include Creative Commons licences (http://creativecommons.org/, [211, 212]), and the UK's Open Government Licence (OGL — http://www.nationalarchives.gov.uk/doc/open-government-licence/), which, to take it as an example, allows users to copy, publish, transmit, distribute, adapt and exploit (commercially) the data, as long as they "acknowledge the source of the Information by including any attribution statement specified by the Information Provider(s) and, where possible, provide a link to this licence." Note that populating the Web with open data demands both social and technological methods. Technology affords access to the data, while the licence removes legal barriers from its reuse.

Open data will live or die by its usefulness, of course. Berners-Lee [42] sets out a 5* rating system that describes how useful data is that has been published online, in cumulative steps as follows:

- * Make your data available on the Web under an open licence.
- ** Make it available as structured data.
- *** Use non-proprietary formats
- **** Use linkable formats.
- ***** Link it to others' data.

So, as an example, a dataset released as a pdf file, with the data perhaps embedded in text, tables or diagrams, would earn one star if it was published online under an open licence. The format is not important, but the licence is the basic condition of open data. Each increase of a star increases the utility of the data. Structured data can be processed directly, unlike the pdf which would have to be scraped — an example would be releasing an Excel spreadsheet. A non-proprietary format does not tie the user into particular software packages (such as Microsoft's Excel), and an example would be CSV. As we have seen above, one linkable format is RDF, and the advantages of four-star and five-star data are the possibilities following the use of the Web's functionality to, e.g., reuse data, bookmark it, merge it and discover new sources. The rating system of Berners-Lee [42] makes it evident that open data can be part of the LDW (if it is five-star data), but need not be (if it is three stars or less). Four-star data is also not part of the LDW, but requires nothing more than appropriate linking to connect it.

The value of open data follows from the assumption that more data produces better inference, yet as with linked data there are challenges to its adoption. One obvious application area is science where easily available data are helpful both with theory construction and with testing and validation of others' results [64]. Open data is especially valuable in interdisciplinary areas. Such synthetic, collaborative disciplines (which include Web Science, and also ecology, climate science, demography and information science) will benefit from the ability to gather and combine data from authoritative sources across the sciences.

Yet important desiderata for such data nonetheless go beyond the representational aspects of the 5* system, and speak to the importance of practice, management, regulation and other social processes. Whereas linked data have a broadly common ethos of publication, open data covers a greater range of types of data (which may include linked data), and is obtainable from heterogeneous sources. Information metadata are required; as with linked data, provenance issues loom large, both in terms of the original data, and the new data derived from it. Culture also matters. At the moment, it is hard to mutualise the costs of publishing open data (typically, one organisation takes on the burden of collecting the data, and publishing merely gives it an extra overhead and no clear financial benefit). Traditionally, a scientific paper concentrates on the narrative of the discovery, and the data is secondary; data archiving in scientific papers would be a way around that problem [360]. For reviews of the issues in particular communities, see e.g., Refs. [268, 303].

It has been argued that open data is an important way to empower people to achieve their goals and manage their own affairs independently of government, the state or powerful corporations with their own agendas. For instance, Meggiolaro et al. [244] claim that equitable and gender-aware land governance can be facilitated by online platforms using open data, using the Land Portal (http://landportal.info/) as an example. Hall et al. [146] argue that open data can be an extremely potent asset for charities and non-profit organisations, in two ways. First of all, they gain access to data beyond their own databases. Second, if they move toward publishing their data, the discipline that imposes is valuable in increasing the effectiveness of data management generally. Hall et al. [146] make the point that the extra commitment of publishing open data is important both for improving the coverage of publicly-available data (thereby benefiting all), and for creating valuable network effects to help foster growing communities of organisations. The tangible and immediate benefit for an organisation of publishing open data may be small, but the longer term effects will become visible both within and without the organisation.

Open data is a factor in the development of the LDW, in that government data (which is often open) already makes up about a sixth of the linked data out there. However, it is driven to a large extent by political considerations — the urge to create transparent government, to introduce accountability in government agencies, and to open the way to private sector provision of innovative services. Open data therefore bestrides the engineering of the LDW, and also the macro-effects of the Web in society, where it is transforming politics, which will be the subject of the next subsection.

6.3 Technology and the Transformation of Politics

Organisational forms depend for their viability on the technology available to implement them. This is an important factor in many areas of economics and political science. For instance, many theories of political action with laudable aims (such as to create a more just or more egalitarian distribution of resources, or to increase liberty) depend on particular technological possibilities to implement them. The connection between technology and patterns of governance is a powerful theme squarely in the realm of Web Science. Patrick Dunleavy and colleagues have argued that forms of governance have followed social, economic and technological changes, and that the development and social diffusion of the Web have created opportunities for governments (certainly in the rich democracies) to innovate and to save money at the same time [113]. In this subsection, we will consider ways in which governments have sought to transform themselves and the Web, looking in Section 6.3.1 at ways in which Web technologies have been co-opted for traditional governmental functions, and then at initiatives exploiting some of the newer Web technologies, including the LDW and open data (Section 6.3.2). Section 6.3.3 revisits the perennial theme of privacy, which was briefly touched upon in Berners-Lee et al. [44, pp. 104–106]. Certainly there is evidence of a divergence between ideas of government (cf. [321]), leading to different ideas about how to meet the various challenges that government poses for technology, including how to represent, publish, integrate and discover knowledge, how to manage change, how to deal with privacy, and how to facilitate service provision on the Web [321, pp. 845–864].

6.3.1 Digital Era Governance

Dunleavy and co-workers [112, 113, 232] were originally moved to problematise, study and critique the theory of 'New Public Management' (NPM), a drive to slim down traditional governmental structures, disaggregate functions and provide incentives for service providers, while putting service contracts out to competitive tender to eliminate bureaucratic monopolies. NPM's motivation was based on the neoliberal ideology of thinkers such as Hayek and Friedman, and took the opportunity of new digital technological affordances of the 1980s and 1990s to map out a programme of change. Dunleavy et al. write that as public affection for and familiarity with Web technology (particular Web 2.0) have increased via such applications as social media, SNSs and wikis, then governmental organisations have been able to take advantage of new forms of interaction including P2P, crowdsourcing, network effects and informal associations to supersede NPM. They call the use of such technologies *Digital Era Governance* (DEG).

With DEG, state–private sector boundaries are blurred, and governments are both pressed, and seek the opportunity, to innovate to exploit social dispositions to use new technologies. The mystique of government, and its privilege of 'owning' debate and making decisions 'behind closed doors' are disappearing, and being replaced by 'open book' governance, transparency and open data initiatives. In a period of austerity following the financial crisis of 2008, policymakers are keen on the increases in efficiency, while as acceptance of authority has declined across most of the rich democracies, the idea that voters and citizens can 'buy in' to policy by being directly involved in its creation is also attractive.

The DEG model moves the agenda on from NPM, reimposing the holistic view of government that NPM rejected. Organisational structures are reintegrated (albeit more flexibly than in traditional hierarchical, bureaucratic and corporatist models) to take processes out of silos and create new partnerships to work under a governmental umbrella (for example, providing 'one stop shops' for citizens). Needs-based holism drives service provision through client-based structures, and the Web becomes a prime mover for both data gathering (citizen to government) and service provision (government to citizen). Intermediaries between service providers and citizens are eliminated (in some countries, this reduces the opportunities for corruption).

However, efforts to optimise the use of Web technology are somewhat patchy [321]. This is an issue in the context of Dunleavy et al.'s [113] more powerful claim that their model is not only descriptive, but also normative — that is, that the DEG model not only describes how government is evolving, but also specifies how it *ought* to evolve. In that context, it is a species of the Web Science control problem of trying to cause and direct change. Recent work on e-government, however, has shown that interoperability and re-engineering problems can interfere with the effectiveness of government services online. Studies have highlighted the need for standards to support interoperability, security and privacy following amalgamation of databases and services, and process re-engineering to optimise the benefits of shifting governmental services online. Though several countries are making progress, there is a growing divide across the globe between those nations with strong traditions in IT, and those without. E-government seems to be more successfully implemented with a holistic cross-government perspective, rather than a more siloed, sector-based approach. E-services provided by government still have a relatively low uptake [353].

Despite the opportunities that are available, governments can be reluctant, or feel unable, to follow through, as Peristeras et al. describe:

> Governmental agencies still publish public-sector information (PSI) using a wide variety of nonstandardized and proprietary formats. The sheer volume and wealth of PSI make the potential benefits of reusing, combining, and processing this information quite apparent. However, agencies typically first express reluctance to make their data available, for various cultural, political, and institutional reasons. So, they keep their legacy systems, and the information stored there, fenced and isolated. Even if they decide to move on and free their data, the different data formats, the lack of commonly agreed-upon metadata, and the absence of standardized vocabularies and definitions result in a huge bulk of practically useless data [290].

Rendering this mountain of data tractable is a vital first step towards semantically-enabled government services, and would be an important gain in its own right.

Implementation of e-government services of all kinds is usually seen as a stage by stage process of increasing political and technological sophistication. Layne and Lee [203], in common with other commentators, set out a four-stage process, of which the first is cataloguing, creating an online presence, putting government information on the Web, creating downloadable forms etc, giving a one-way communication (broadcasting) facility. In the second stage, the internal government information systems are connected with the online interfaces, so citizens can transact with government, make requests, provide information, fill in forms etc, making communication two-way. The third stage is one of vertical integration, where local systems are linked to higher-level systems with related functionality. The result for the citizen is a 'one-stop shop' which appears seamless. Resources of greater value than information can be exchanged. The final stage is horizontal integration, where systems are integrated across functions, services become ubiquitous, and the individual departments of government become increasingly irrelevant from the point of view of the citizen, who just picks up the services she needs from a single portal.

It is instructive to consider these stages in terms of the emergence of structures out of lower-level interactions that provides the theme for this monograph. Layne and Lee's first stage provides a set of fixed structures for local action on the part of individual citizens; the government dictates the methods of interaction and the citizen has little input. However, the second, third and fourth stages introduce feedback loops where the actual structures of government can be influenced by local action (as well as vice versa). The rich feedback that citizens provide can cause change in government structures themselves, so that behind the scenes actual institutions begin to alter their internal structure and external connections in order to service citizens' requirements more effectively. In particular, it is the third and fourth stages which are genuinely transformative of government information infrastructure, to implement Dunleavy et al.'s idea of DEG.

However, it is fair to say (a) that very few e-government systems have been genuinely transformative [353], and (b) that the application of cutting edge Web technology (particularly Semantic Web technology) in this space has been more in the realm of prototypes or proofs of concept than fully-fledged delivered systems or procedures. It has proven harder than some might have anticipated for enough control to be exercised over either the technological development, or the institutional structures, to implement digital era governance in accordance with the structural ideals that we understand from technologies like linked data and the Semantic Web [321, 361]. This is another Web Science research problem in the area of indirect control.

Interestingly, the use of technology in politics has its strongest drivers in the United States, where campaigning for office is driven by individuals with deep pockets, or targeted interest groups. In the US, the Obama and Romney campaigns of 2012 (plus the campaigns of other candidates such as Newt Gingrich, Michele Bachmann, Rick Santorum, Rick Perry, etc.) were orchestrated by the candidates themselves, rather than the Democratic or the Republican Parties. This allows innovation and entrepreneurialism to replace the inertia of other nations' party-based systems, with the Web featuring prominently since the insurgent campaign in the Democratic primaries of 2004 by Howard Dean, who used technology to combine a platform for populist views with impressive fundraising capabilities. In the close race of 2012, it is plausible to suggest that Obama's use of technology was decisive. His seamless sociotechnical combination of big data crunching to establish patterns of support and voting, social networking to galvanise supporters and to raise money, and a large number of physical offices to support volunteers knocking on doors, bids fair to be cast as a social machine in the sense that we have used the term in this monograph [272].

6.3.2 Linked Open Government Data

An alternative approach to the delivery of public services mandated by government is to take a more hands-off approach, with governments exploiting some of the technologies we have outlined in Section 6.2, and especially Section 6.2.4, to create linked open government data. The intuition is very simple — put government data online and allow users free access in order to create and deliver innovative services. Such services do not need to replace government-provided, or government-procured, services, but could sit alongside them. They could be monetised or delivered *pro bono*. The main point is that entrepreneurs and designers would have not only the opportunity but also the knowledge resources to produce useful services. In such a world, there would be no rent-seeking based on exclusive access agreements or restrictive licences. Developers would have a level playing field, and would have to compete on creativity. This approach contrasts with the more paternal view that has characterised e-government and semantic e-government in the past [321, 361].

Government data is an important source of open data. It is abundant, of good provenance and of reasonable if variable quality. As government data, it is relevant to people's concerns. It is a means of holding governments to account. Most importantly, there is a strong case that citizens have a right to it. Governments are given democratic legitimacy to collect data via the votes of their citizens, and have the resources to do it via receipts from their taxpayers. Therefore (modulo questions of national security, personal data, etc.), there seems little reason why citizens shouldn't have access to the data, or services built on them, if these could be socially or economically valuable. Open government data, in a sense, formalises and liberalises the freedom of information legislation operative in many nations.

Many nations, particularly the United Kingdom and the United States of America, are working to develop their open data programmes, and results are starting to flow. The US Digital Government Strategy (http://www.whitehouse.gov/sites/default/files/omb/egov/digital-government/digital-government.html) moves government "from managing 'documents' to managing discrete pieces of open data and content which can be tagged, shared, secured, mashed up and presented in the way that is most useful for the consumer of that information." Data.gov (http://www.data.gov/) was established in 2009 as a central repository for open data, and has fostered communities of practice using structured open linked data around general topics such as business, health and energy, and specific problems such as restoring ecosystems following the Deepwater Horizon oil spill in the Gulf of Mexico. The Linked Open Government Data (LOGD) portal, http://logd.tw.rpi.edu/, provides open data converted to RDF, links to other linked data resources such as DBpedia, and includes demos, tools and search [157]. In the UK data.gov.uk (http://data.gov.uk/), launched in January 2010, contains government datasets from many domains. Public Data Principles (http://data.gov.uk/library/public-data-principles) enshrine UK government open data policy and contain a commitment to linked data.

It is fair to say that most open government data is two- or three-star data in the Berners-Lee [42] rating system, yet the real gains are likely to come from five-star (linked) data [315]. For example, the European Commission has an Interoperability Solutions programme (http://ec.europa.eu/isa/) for public administration, and has an open data portal, http://open-data.europa.eu/open-data/, providing access to nearly 6000 datasets (of which 97% are three-star statistical data from Eurostat), with metadata in RDF.

There have been concerns about the costs of publishing linked data to create seamless interoperable services. The investment in re-engineering may look daunting in terms of initial cost, and possibly even in terms of expected benefit. This leads to a pragmatic issue about whether it is better to use a 'top down' approach to conversion, engaging a powerful person or administrative body high up in the hierarchy which prescribes methods, determines resources, and incentivises change, or alternatively to support 'bottom up' processes allowing interoperability to be negotiated by smaller units at the leaf nodes of the hierarchy engaging in information sharing, maybe in bilateral arrangements, culminating in the emergence of a shared approach which then can be formalised.

In a complex and fragmented domain such as e-government, some bottom up processes will be required [365], because so many different cultures and practices, formal and informal, will be involved. Equally, top down pressure will also be required (a) to ensure that those departments reluctant to change still undergo the process, (b) to ensure consistency between approaches and to avoid reinventing the wheel (e.g., by sharing of ontologies), (c) to steer re-engineering strategically, (d) to provide rewards and incentives for good practice, and (e) to gather, disseminate and mandate best practice [321].

Governments and data users should be tolerant of complexity. As argued above, multiple URIs are inevitable in a decentralised webby world. In general, generating a new URI is not the solution to a world with too many URIs, but equally governments and pan-government institutions such as the EU are well-placed to be authoritative with data representation. Once more there is a balance to be struck between standards and decentralisation, but governments are rather better placed to support standardisation where it is valuable [319]. An official URI for each significant object or concept would liberate information from the silos, as well as carrying a great deal of weight given the quantity and authority of government data around. Particularly crucial data, core reference data, connects a lot of datasets, including geodata, postcodes, businesses and contracts [320]. For example, there are a number of linked geodatasets designed to bring together data with a spatial element [331, 289].

In general, any approach to providing linked open government data must somehow try to resolve the five challenges identified by Ding et al. [105], each of which probably requires pushes from both directions (see also [320] for commentary on these).

- More data is needed in order to get over the barriers to entry to the LDW, to show the benefits of reuse.
- More links need to be generated, for example via backlinking (following a unidirectional link backwards, on the intuition that if A is relevant to B, B is relevant to A).
- Reusable identity and provenance materials are required.
- Data needs to be accessible, with good browsers and vocabulary standardisation.
- Collaborative international networks are needed to develop user communities and common approaches.

There is a another pragmatic argument for using semantic and linked data technologies in e-government, that even if costs are perceived to be high, the technology is an important means to transformation. If the aim is to produce horizontally and vertically integrated e-government, a semantic representation of government data, maximising the use of external data and also releasing government data to the outside world will be important steps towards that goal. The benefits and incentives are clearer than one might imagine; Shadbolt and O'Hara [319] argue that the experience of the UK government in producing linked data has produced internal efficiency (it is easier for a government department or agency to consume its own linked data than to integrate data by hand), helped set authoritative standards (for instance, as many concepts are defined by legislation, the reproduction of UK legislation as linked data on http://www.legislation.gov.uk/ allows URIs to refer to those concepts as they appear in law, allowing complex inference over them — [351]), and generally widened the scope of what can be done with open data. On the other hand, as Kone et al. [196] argue, the Semantic Web and linked data cannot do everything; culturally, cooperation will still need to be fostered, for example over standard reference ontologies. The W3C's interest group on e-government has published a working draft on how to publish open data [37], and recommends the following steps: (i) publish data in its raw form if it is structured and can be extracted from the document; (ii) create a catalogue with documentation of what it available; (iii) then convert the data so it is human- and machine-readable, with semantics, metadata and URIs.

The particular case of small governments has also been studied [194]; such governments are thought to lack the management and re-engineering resources to improve semantic interoperability of distributed e-government services and resources. The level of support required is large, and the initial costs can also be risky to take on. It follows that quick wins and a lowering of ambition (for example, not using a single elaborate ontology, but multiple overlapping small-scale ontologies) will be important factors here [7]. Klischewski's work in Schleswig-Holstein, a small German state with 1000 heterogeneous municipalities, revealed that maintaining up-to-date and standardised information bases locally for use by the state government is hard (small municipalities do not have the workforce), while central databases are inefficient [195]. Therefore, any central e-government application has to obtain the required information from heterogeneous local sources. This requires motivating such municipalities to cooperate, which in turn demands a deep and sympathetic identification of their requirements and constraints, and transfer of resources downwards (e.g., for provision of new methodologies and tools).

6.3.3 Privacy and Surveillance

There are many important political issues for which Web Science can supply important data, such as privacy [275], net neutrality [267], democracy [80, 238] and how to regulate the cloud [288]. However, space precludes long discussions about all these thorny issues. As an example of a political issue, privacy serves extremely well, given the powerful effects that the LDW, open data and new types of politics may have on the privacy of the individual [270].

The question of what commitments people make, and should be expected to make, and what they should be expected to surrender, when they shop, blog, search or communicate online has been fraught for years. On the one hand, there is a panoply of data protection measures which date back to the age of standalone databases, enshrined for example in the 1995 EU Data Protection Directive, and as a result of that in the laws of each of the 28 EU nations. These are hardly perfect protections for individuals' privacy [270], but do have an effect. Taken literally, data protection legislation on the European model would make it very hard for surveillance-based business models to take hold. On the other hand, there is a clear demand for free services and environments (such as SNSs), which certainly need to be funded from somewhere. On the axiom that 'if something seems to be free, it isn't', it should be clear for users that some kind of *quid pro quo* is in operation, such that some revenue is accruing for whoever provides the free environment. And the biggest resource created by online activity is the trail of socialising and purchasing that an individual leaves behind. The issue is complicated by data and document sharing being embedded in the Web's (and Internet's) protocols — this is not simply a matter of governance, but a technical question whose answers will affect the engineering of the Web itself.

Thus the framing of this problem around privacy has been challenged on a number of related fronts, some of which accept (or even welcome) technological intrusion, and others which resist. Some commentators simply assert that social norms are changing, often driven by technological change, which will inevitably result in the failure of 'old hat' techniques or tools to protect citizens or consumers. Such arguments are generally made by those with a stake in the system as it is growing [269, 162], such as the former chairman of Sun Microsystems, Scott McNeally, who famously asserted that our privacy was gone and that we should "get over it." Marc Zuckerberg of Facebook has also uttered similar ideas, while much of Google's activity seems to be premised on the notion that they serve the public good. The general good of data sharing, whether for social purposes or to benefit the individual, has been argued cogently [168]. In each case, the techno-deterministic line is that privacy norms are changing. This takes some of the sting out of arguments such as Nissenbaum's [265] that information should be shared and distributed only according to the norms covering distinct social contexts, because if those norms are changing so, necessarily, would privacy practices. Some have argued that common law legal protections exploiting the 'reasonable expectation of privacy' are being eroded as the efficiency of technologies of search, surveillance and data mining increases [186, 235, 237]. Hetcher [160] uses game theory and the concept of 'norm entrepreneurialism' (the promotion by civic society of specific norms or practices) to make a more optimistic argument that the practices of organisations on the Web can (and have) been changed by concerted identification and exposure of harmful practices.

Meanwhile, it can be difficult to identify specific harms that have occurred to people as a result of invasions of their privacy. One way of exposing harm is to examine particular theories of privacy to determine why it is important, such as the detailed philosophical argument of Rössler [305] that privacy is a guarantor of autonomy in a liberal society. Unfortunately, these arguments are harder to make when it is clear that SNSs allow users to make play with different identities and to experiment with disclosure, in ways that would be ruled out if there were stricter controls on what such sites could do [119, 175, 242, 330]. Furthermore, the movement toward the 'quantified self', or 'lifelogging', where people gather and monitor their own data ([34], and http://quantifiedself.com/), is also likely to exacerbate privacy concerns, not only when such data is shared (which [34] advise against), but also because security and control of the data cannot always be guaranteed [12, 278].

Chew et al. [90], writing as researchers for Google, set out three particular types of harm from SNSs: lack of control over activity streams, unwelcome linkage of different facets of identity, and merging of social graphs. In a similar vein, Vihavainen et al. [359] also identify three "recurring privacy-related issues": insensitivity to situational demands, inadequate control of nuance and veracity, and inability to control disclosure with service providers and third parties (for more on the harms, see also [36, pp. 494–496]). The obvious counter to this kind of analysis is that these 'harms' are being perceived by those 'harmed' either as not harmful, or as outweighed by other benefits. If researchers in academe (or in companies like Google whose interests diverge from those of the major SNSs) can dictate to people what is and is not harmful independently of their perceptions, one might ask where individuals' autonomy stands now. Stronger evidence of general harm may arise when surveillance turns into profiling, where assumptions are made about people based on (a fraction of) their online activities; these assumptions may discriminate and seriously restrict autonomy. Nevertheless, the data protection instruments with which we are familiar may not be the best methods for ensuring that profiling does not cause harm [161].

Some argue that privacy is simply the wrong concept. It has a peculiar history out of liberalism, which does not capture the full impact of technology on the life of the individual. Its value is subjective, and yet is based on a particular understanding of human rights (often as articulated in Article 8 of the European Convention on Human Rights). It is not a stable attitude, as shown by studies in behavioural economics which reveal what has been called the 'privacy paradox', whereby people's behaviour and their professed attitudes to privacy are in contradiction [1]. In all this, it fails to capture important power relationships, abilities to discriminate and the harms to groups of people that the wider concept of surveillance covers [35, 36, 223, 310]. Additionally, it is worth noting that the generalised increase in access to information across entire populations, as exploited by movements such as the quantified self, has led to a generalised and democratised increase in surveillance. *Sousveillance*, as it has been called, is another way in which privacy is eroded simply by an increase in the deployment of surveillance technology (cf. [69, 228]). In many cases, the encroaching technology is based on particular types of device, but the Web is implicated in particular via SNSs and the gathering of data about clickthroughs and commercial applications.

In the face of these arguments, some have argued that the main aim should not be to protect privacy, but rather to increase transparency.

Many business models (and many social goods) are protected by sharing data; many free and innovative services are made possible because the data that they generate can be exploited. Google's advertising model is perhaps the most obvious example although they are legion; the value of Google's search engine to its users is incalculable, but it has to be funded, and the funds come from advertising based on surveillance. Stifling such innovation would be counter-productive, goes this argument, even if it was possible in an age where copying and aggregation are trivially easy. However, that is no reason why the exploitation of data should be covert. Making the use of data transparent would make it possible to make those who use data accountable for their usage of it, thereby allowing sanctions to be applied to them if they do not repair harms [374]. Hildebrandt [161] argues that being informed about profiling and the potential consequences of that is a useful protection against the surveillance/profiling industry. It may also be possible for individuals to demand a share of the profits from the use of their data [276], while commercial models are emerging that allow individuals to exert greater control over their data without stifling innovative services around that [153]. Nevertheless, there are still a number of complex issues surrounding the regulation of the right to be notified about surveillance, and the devil will no doubt be in the detail [98].

6.4   Personal Data Stores: Data Management for the Individual

As the Web and the wider society change, technology is also creating opportunities for the individual. As personal data starts to appear in large quantities, this not only creates a resource for governments and corporations, but also for the data subjects themselves, if they had access to it in their Personal Data Stores (PDSs). Search terms, cookies, location data, tweets and clickstreams can be useful for individuals and consumers who generate them, as a record of their lives and transactions which could be empowering or even monetised. This is an important area where control of the Web's development, which we have so far considered in terms of macro structure, could positively influence lives of individuals.

Indeed, there is a whole new paradigm building around the notion of the empowerment of data subjects. Searls [312] argues that free markets need free customers, but draws attention to the fact that the traditional area where customer data is handled, Customer Relations Management, uses slavery-based imagery to describe its functions: acquire, control, retain, manage, lock in and own. Customers are a stock to be managed, in this imagery. Yet much data is actually created by customers themselves, and they consent to the use of much more; they could be active participants in the use of their data to create economic value [178]. There will be important opportunities, and potential costs, as the technology to support Personal Data Management (PDM) begins to be developed [162].

6.4.1 Data

In European data protection law, data subjects have the right to inspect data held about them, but in practice this right is rarely exercised and is difficult to administer. Indeed, when data is provided to the subject, it is often produced on paper and for a fee — nothing about data protection law implies that the data supplied should be machine readable, and so it can be made deliberately hard to process. Yet increases in computing power, especially in the devices owned by consumers, has led to initiatives to make individuals' access to data held about them more routine. In the US, 'smart disclosure' encompasses the commercial world and that of the federal government, and there have been over a million attempts to — in the slogan used by the health-data-related blue button programme — 'download my data'. In France, the Mesinfos initiative is running pilot schemes to discover opportunities for applications and services (http://fing.org/?-MesInfos-les-donnees-personnelles-&lang=en).

Perhaps the most advanced programme is the UK Midata scheme [315]. This is a government programme to get the private sector to allow individuals access to data held about them, to provide a safe environment and safe practices for individuals to use data about themselves for their own purposes, and to encourage innovative services to develop around the use of such data. Areas of likely progress include providing individuals with an understanding of their patterns of consumption (and possibly to be able to change them for the better), allowing more informed purchasing decisions, facilitating group negotiation on prices and combining the data with data from other sources (including open data). The government has extracted specific commitments from private sector actors to develop online 'personal data inventories' (PDIs) describing the types of data an organisation holds about each customer. The proposal is that a consumer would log in to a secure website where their PDI would contain a simple explanation of each category of data available and whether and how it could be accessed.

The details of the programme are described in Ref. [315], but from the Web Science point of view, we need to understand how this affects business models which depend on data hoarding and artificial scarcity. Important issues to be addressed include privacy, security and common standards. Where does liability lie in the event that data is misused by the subject? Can vulnerable individuals be protected? What will be the effect of reflexive behavioural insight — the idea that you can know a great deal about yourself? Could one 'nudge' oneself — be both Pavlov and the dog simultaneously?

Most obviously, there is a need to pick through a regulatory minefield, especially where European and US approaches differ greatly. The law around personal data is complex and varies from jurisdiction to jurisdiction. 'Ownership' of data assets, because of the nonrivalrous nature of data, is not definitive. For these and other reasons legislative protection is often cast in terms of privacy, which in Europe is taken as a fundamental right (Article 8 of the European Convention). This has been given a broad interpretation in Strasbourg by the European Court of Human Rights, and drove the development of the EU's Data Protection Directive to regulate the processing of personal data within the member states, and facilitate a single market for the free movement of such data. However, a new directive is in preparation at the moment, and the process has been somewhat tortuous — it is not at the time of writing clear how far the new directive will support personal access to data, or how it will affect the balance between privacy and markets. Nevertheless, an update of the directive is necessary, as the existing one was built for the pre-Web world of standalone databases — it does not transfer very well to the Web and will be even less well adapted to a world of Cloud-based computing services where an individual's data may be collected in one jurisdiction, processed in another and stored in a third. In particular, the directive is not terribly relevant for a world of PDM in which individuals could be their own data controllers. The UK, in the context of midata, has side-stepped the uncertainty relating to the revision of the directive and given itself the powers to compel firms to release data to individuals in machine-readable format.

Although legislation in the EU and the US is based on the OECD principles of data protection from the 1980s, the two jurisdictions have different approaches. In the US until 2012 there was no comprehensive federal legislation for data protection, and restrictions on the use of data were applied only to specific sectors such as healthcare, education, communications and financial services or, in the case of online data collection, to children. However, in February 2012 the White House's Consumer Privacy Bill of Rights created for the first time an overarching framework for protecting consumer information and privacy rights to their personal data, containing many of the OECD principles. It may be that pressures from technology are actually pushing two very different regulatory systems closer together, which will have profound effects on data markets and on the individual's sense of privacy and control.

6.4.2   Architectures

The picture that has been building up through this monograph is of a Web increasingly engaged with offline life, where the online/offline distinction is decreasingly meaningful, documents are giving way to data, and control is devolved to individuals or smaller groups as far as possible — in short, a much more complex environment where we cannot rely on simple command-and-control hierarchies to determine the use of information. What infrastructure could underpin decentralised and user-centric data services, scalable and flexible enough to deal with data of varying granularity and structure from a single statement to an entire graph, and futureproofed as far as possible against entirely novel schemata? For an analysis of the most important sharing capabilities, see Ref. [356].

The ProjectVRM group (http://cyber.law.harvard.edu/projectvrm/ Main_Page) has studied the feasibility of decentralised approaches under user control from sociotechnical and economic perspectives. Their analysis and continued discussion (blogs.law.harvard.edu/vrm) have shown that the decentralisation of personal information, driven by cost-incentives and need to comply with data protection regulation, have indicated a significant shift towards greater personal control of data in the next decade (see also Ref. [162]). Implementations, however, are in early stages. Mydex [153], a Community Interest Company in the UK, has produced a proof-of-concept PDS based on the Java platform, called Higgins (http://www.eclipse. org/higgins/). Similar open source personal data storage containers include The Locker Project (http://lockerproject.org/), data.fm (http://data.fm/), ownCloud (http://owncloud.org/), and OpenStack (http://www.openstack.org/), which all provide various degrees of easy-to-set-up 'personal cloud' software to store and host content on the user's own server on the Web.

Although built with the same goal, these PDS platforms exhibit several differences. Higgins and Openstack are generic schema-agnostic data containers that provide simple storage and retrieval APIs for this data, typically via a RESTful API. The Locker Project, Owncloud, and Diaspora, meanwhile are social-network inspired and centred around a fixed set of simple data types, such as hosting files, status messages, photos, and calendar events. The data.fm project provides a platform to create linked data in a generic read/write Web style. Opera Unite (http://unite.opera.com/overview/) goes a step further by giving users access to a 'Web server' within their browser, which could be used to share media with other users. However, development ceased on Opera Unite in 2012 as it failed to find an audience [343]. Platforms are often either insufficiently schema-agnostic for general function, or fail to support the functionality associated with sharing, such as keeping subscribers informed or principled access control. There were also some security issues (for instance, Opera Unite exposed the file system to outside applications).

Another desideratum for a Web sharing architecture is that it provides seamless access to data available in the decentralised setting.

The Nepomuk Semantic Desktop project [142] created a group collaboration architecture using Semantic Web technologies and peer-to-peer networks. Although Nepomuk is ontology-driven and supports group collaboration, it is geared towards the desktop experience rather than a cloud-based Web experience. The increasing obsolescence of the desktop model as opposed to the cloud means that decentralisation needs to be taken seriously at all levels; PrPl [313] is a decentralised social networking infrastructure that allows users to share personal data in a peer-to-peer network through intermediaries called 'butlers'. Even so, PrPl needs more than open Web standards; it requires applications to be written using a specialised language, whereas a fully decentralised architecture would be language-agnostic.

WebBox [356] is a standards-based, application-generic, schema-agnostic secure platform for structured data sharing with a focus on scalability and usability. It provides messaging, authentication, and access control, and exploits existing Semantic Web technology to allow applications from any source, without prescribing a particular language or access protocol (applications communicate with the WebBox server via a SPARQL endpoint). WebBox extends the role of the Web server from a document publishing platform to one that fundamentally supports distributed collaboration on data artefacts, specifically RDF resources — and shows that this can be achieved without the need for major reinvention. This is an implementation of Socially-Aware Cloud Storage [43, 46] in which social-sharing Web applications access a user-controlled data space for private storage and shared resources, entirely under the user's control. Thus, unlike existing centralised sharing platforms where data and applications are inextricably tied, data can be used by multiple applications and services, and shared directly between peers. From a user's perspective, data can be managed in a single location, resulting in less fragmentation and redundancy, and easier access. Moreover, this ensures that personal data can be maintained independently of applications, ensuring its longevity and sustainability.

Such an architecture which takes decentralisation seriously at all levels will allow greater control for the individual of his or her own store of data. This opens the door for a much richer and more personalised interaction with data on the part of individuals and communities, which will be an important factor in the development of what we refer to here as social machines.

6.5 Social Machines

The Web has been, by and large, a democratic technology, taking power away from those in authority and redistributing it further down the pyramid. Of course we should not take this progress toward democracy as inevitable, as commentators like Morozov [256] are right to remind us. Equally, we must beware of pessimism — every bit as much a species of determinism as techno-optimism.

If control of the Web is slowly getting out of the hands of policy-makers, we must still consider its effects on individuals, civic society and communities. Here there is space, and evidence, for optimism [174]. In Section 1.1, we introduced the idea of *social machines* — partially programmable sociotechnical interactions between people and digital devices. The social machine becomes a potential locus for control for individuals and small groups which probably do not want to change the Web, and probably do not want to change the whole of society. However, they do want to influence their own environment and to exploit the devices with which they are familiar in their own interests.

6.5.1 Precursors of Social Machines: Social Computing Technologies

Social machines build on an important line of development that the Web has facilitated. Computers were once conceived as logical automata, or Turing machines, but this narrow characterisation has evolved into one sensitive to the social context of their use. The emergence of 'computer-supported collaborative work' [143] is representative of the early phases of this trend. This initial concept has evolved into the broader field of 'Computer-Supported Collaboration' (CSC).

Through Web 2.0 and the Mobile Web principles and technologies, the Web is continuing its development as a global platform for information access and sharing characterised by growth of the amount of content available online and in the extent of mass participation in the creation of content, contributions to software and the use of the

Web for other social purposes. This trend towards 'prosumerism' is incentivising more and more adopters in the public and private sector. Governments and enterprises are not only becoming active in open initiatives, but encouraging the participation of their customers and employees in taking decisions relating to organisational management, product development, service offerings, and policy formulation. A number of related but not synonymous terms have appeared to refer to the ways people interact with each other and with applications: 'wisdom of the crowds', 'collective intelligence', 'open innovation', 'crowdsourcing', 'human computation', and 'social computing'.

Wisdom of the crowds [337] refers to a principle for decision making that takes into account the information and opinions of a group of people rather than individuals. Specific technologies, notably Web 2.0, have made it possible for such processes to be carried out at scales inconceivable in the past, and to involve diverse and geographically distributed participants. A similar concept, more broadly scoped, is collective intelligence, groups of individuals doing things collectively that would require intelligence were an individual to carry them out [227].

One of the direct consequences of the popularity of such concepts was a stronger investment worldwide in open innovation, which can be seen as an application of the concept to business environments, or as a 'a paradigm that assumes that firms can and should use external ideas as well as internal ideas, and internal and external paths to market, as the firms look to advance their technology' [89, p. xxiv]. At a more general level, this kind of creativity could be leveraged in almost any domain which benefits from diversity, whilst at the same time ensuring real-time access to a potentially infinite pool of skills and resources not available before the advent of social computing technologies [204, 341, 342]. The term crowdsourcing is typically associated with this larger collection of situations, in which 'a job traditionally performed by a designated agent [is outsourced] to an undefined, generally large group of people in the form of an open call' [165]. Human computation applies human processing power to tackle technical tasks that computers (still) find challenging [362, 363, 364], typically in areas such as visual, audio, and natural language understanding. These kinds of task are an important part of today's crowdsourcing landscape, in particular on so-called 'microtask' platforms such as Amazon's Mechanical Turk (https://www.mturk.com/) or CrowdFlower (http://crowdflower.com/), which offer small financial rewards to an anonymous crowd engaged with atomic units of work that take in the range of seconds to minutes to complete.

Social computing is an area of computer science that refers to systems that support 'the gathering, representation, processing, use, and dissemination of information that is distributed across social collectivities such as teams, communities, organisations, and markets' [285, 284]. As such, compared to the general concept of CSC, social computing puts a greater emphasis on the information management capabilities of groups and communities, and less on the way these capabilities emerge as a joint effort.

6.5.2 Social Machines and Web Science

Figure 1.2 in Section 1.1 implies a pattern of growth of both the community of users and of the number of devices each user has access to which goes beyond the various ideas canvassed in Section 6.5.1. This type of sociotechnical distributed system is what we are calling *social machines* [156, 322]. In Section 1.1, Figure 1.2 sketched out the idea of progress toward greater complexity in computation and social interactions, and if we unpack that image as Figure 6.1, we see the potential space for advancement in more detail. We see conventional computation, even in highly complex domains such as air traffic control and climate modelling, on the left hand side, where social complexity is low even if computational complexity is high. Current systems with high social complexity still involve relatively low computational complexity. Crowdsourcing systems, such as the citizen science initiative Galaxy Zoo [220] have a relatively low level of social complexity as well. More complex social arrangements can be found in the co-creation of content, e.g., Wikipedia, and social networking. However, greater complexity can be found, for example, when social network acts as platforms for crowdsourced co-creation of content, as recently happened with the Ushahidi map of election violence in Kenya in 2007 [279], or the reuse of Ushahidi software to create a post-earthquake map of Port-au-Prince

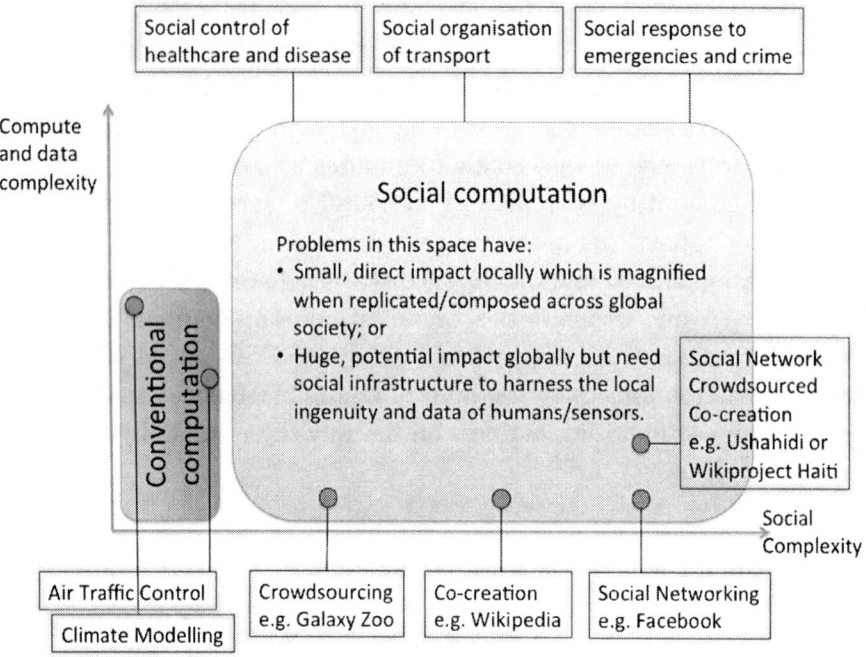

Fig. 6.1 The space of social machines.

in Haiti in 2010 [258]. As we explore this space of social computation, to address perceived issues where there are collective action problems, as with public health, transport or crime, we would expect to find solutions with small impacts locally which will be magnified at scale, as long as the requisite social infrastructure (including Web technologies) is in place.

The idea of a social machine has been implicit throughout the history of the World Wide Web. As Berners-Lee put it in 1999:

> Real life is and must be full of all kinds of social constraint — the very processes from which society arises. Computers can help if we use them to create abstract *social machines* on the Web: processes in which people do the creative work and the machine does the administration ([40, p. 172], Berners-Lee's emphasis).

Many social machines are embedded in SNSs such as Facebook, in which human interactions from organising a birthday party to interacting with a Member of Parliament are underpinned by the engineered environment. Another type of example is a multiplayer online game, where a persistent online environment facilitates interactions concerning virtual resources between real people. A third type is an online poker game, where the resources being played for are real-world, where the players may be human or bots, and where the environment in which the game takes place is engineered around a relatively simple computational model. In such systems, (some of) the social constraints that Berners-Lee talks about, currently norm-driven, are administered by the architecture of the programmed environment.

Such social machines are straightforward (*qua* interaction models), but as the technology is theorised more deeply it is inevitable that more complex systems will be developed, as with the crowdsourced cocreation of content in the Ushahidi examples. A generalised definition of a social computation is provided by Robertson and Giunchiglia [304]:

> A computation for which an executable specification exists but the successful implementation of this specification depends upon computer mediated social interaction between the human actors in its implementation.

In such an environment, self-organisation (partial or full) becomes viable and scalable, while physical objects, agents, contracts, agreements, incentives and other objects can be referred to using URIs. 'Programming' the social computer (as opposed to simply supporting and directing interactions on an engineered environment) and integrating larger numbers of people and machines will become increasingly feasible.

6.5.3 Examples of Social Machines

As a small example of a social machine, consider reCAPTCHA [364]. A CAPTCHA (Completely Automated Public Turing test to tell Computers and Humans Apart), invented by Louis Von Ahn, is the distorted sequence of letters that someone has to type in a box to identify him- or herself as a human (e.g., to buy a ticket online, or to comment on a blog). This is a task that computers cannot do, and so the system stops bots buying thousands of tickets for a concert or sporting event for later resale, and stops spambots leaving spam messages as comments to blogs [363].

Von Ahn extended the idea of the CAPTCHA to create the reCAPTCHA, which uses the same principle to solve another problem. Google (which acquired reCAPTCHA in 2009) uses it to scan older books automatically. The original CAPTCHA device was being used over 200 m times a day, about half a million person-hours of effort. reCAPTCHA puts these person-hours to more productive use, presenting the user who wishes to identify him- or herself as a human with two words, not one. The first is a normal CAPTCHA, and the second is a word from an old book that Optical Character Recognition had failed to identify. If the person succeeds with the first CAPTCHA, then he or she is known to be a human. As humans are reliable at word recognition, the response to the second word as a plausible suggestion of what it is. Presenting the same word to multiple users allows a consensus to emerge.

As another example, Robertson and Giunchiglia [304] use the DARPA balloon challenge of 2009, in which the aim was to find ten weather balloons placed randomly around the US (in nine different states from California to Delaware). The rules of the challenge were intended to support the growth of a network of people taking part in the search, enabling a crowdsourced solution. The means of doing this in the winning solution (from Sandy Pentland at the Massachusetts Institute of Technology) was to set out financial incentives according to a Query Incentive Network Model [192], in which people were incentivised both to look for the balloons and to add more people to the network. Pentland's team began with 4 people, and using social media had recruited over 5000 at the point of completion, which took under ten hours [293].

reCAPTCHA and the DARPA challenge were designed to solve a particular problem, but social machines can, and indeed should [271], solve the problems of the people who constitute them. In such cases, the incentive of the participants is that the machine's smooth functioning is in their own interests. One could imagine, for instance, a set of computer-mediated interactions enabling a community to provide a social response to problems of crime (such as BlueServo, http://www.blueservo.net/, which crowdsources the policing of the Texas–Mexico border), or enabling those suffering from a particular health care problem to pool resources and to offer support and advice to fellow sufferers (such as http://curetogether.com/). There is a growing number of health social machines, as surveyed in detail in [355]. It will be obvious from these examples, particularly BlueServo, that such efforts will not always be uncontroversial. Attempts to crowdsource the identities of the bombers of the Boston Marathon in 2013 bordered on farce, and, although the countercultural website 4chan was prominent in the home-made policing efforts with its so-called '4chan Think Tank', its lamentable efforts were soon parodied elsewhere on the same site [366]. Trust will be a major factor in the success of such machines [271].

6.5.4 Differences Between the Social Machines Concept and Its Precursors

The main difference between social machines and collective intelligence/crowd wisdom is with regard to the extent, complexity and role of automation, as shown in Figure 6.1. In a social machine, human and computational intelligence coalesce in order to achieve a given purpose. While crowd wisdom and collective intelligence focus on identifying the situations in which groups of people perform better than individuals, social machines are concerned with the study and realisation of hybrid systems in which the two types of components co-exist. As such, theoretical and empirical insights from these two related areas are useful to understand the dynamics of the social structures underlying a social machine, but they are definitely not the only ingredient needed to build operational systems. The question of how human and automatic services can be brought together to achieve optimal results, as well as the actual engineering by which a system is developed, tested, and updated are equally important [156, 322].

The key difference between social machines and open innovation and crowdsourcing is at the level of the interaction between the social and the machine-driven processing components. The novelty of the two other approaches lies in their use of a much larger pool of human resources than traditional work environments [298]. There are clear socioeconomic implications that their adopters need to deal with in order to optimise this wealth of resources; technology may be needed to assist specific aspects of crowdsourcing projects from evaluating and rewarding the results produced by the crowd to consolidating and aggregating them into a complete solution. These aspects are equally important for social machines, which, however, also look into the principled combination of human and computational capabilities and the technical means to support them.

In comparison to human computation, social machines cover a wider range of scenarios. Human computation is AI-centric and uses people to perform tasks that computers are not (yet) able to tackle (in terms of accuracy) [298]; by comparison, we see many successful examples of social machines in which the role of machines is rather to facilitate interactions within groups of people or communities of interest.

7

Conclusion

The end crowns all.

Troilus and Cressida, act IV scene v

Understanding the Web is a problem on a par with other complex scientific challenges such as climate change or the human genome. The
requirement for understanding should ideally be accompanied by some
measure of control, which makes Web Science crucial in the future
provision of tools for managing our interactions, our politics, our economics, our entertainment and not least our knowledge and data sharing. The Web is a critical infrastructure that underpins increasingly
many of our transactions, and yet is barely understood by policymakers.

In this paper, we have argued that part of the problem is that many
of the significant phenomena are emergent. Many local actions produce
macro-level patterns at scale, but the causal interactions of these are
somewhat mysterious, partly due to the lack of data, and partly due
to the sheer speed at which change occurs. Yet ultimately, if the Web
is to remain a positive benefit to humanity, as Berners-Lee et al. [44]
argued in this journal at the beginning of the Web Science adventure,
control will have to be applied. Control requires understanding, and

understanding requires a powerful interdisciplinary grasp of the many relevant features that the Web exhibits. The Web, it has been argued, is humanity connected [318], and that phrase certainly dramatises the scale of the problem. As noted in Section 6.1.2 and elsewhere, this means the levels of analysis will always need to include an understanding of the macro context if the number of unintended consequences is to be reduced. The Web Observatory [347], and related exercises [2, 241] will be key tools in that effort (see Section 4.5).

The themes outlined in this paper give form to the Web Science programme, in their coverage of so many social, psychological and technical issues, working towards control. Emergence is a result of the complex interplay of local actions and initiatives, global patterns and feedback. In this paper, in considering local action and the endogenous local variables in the 'system' that we can loosely classify the Web as (Section 3), we focused on the psychology of joining and/or rejecting communities, and the pressures that an individual may feel as a result of new affordances of Web technologies. There is a major debate to be had as to whether these affordances are generally-speaking good or generally-speaking bad, and we have reflected this debate in our discussion. Doubtless a good narrative might be made to defend either proposition, but it remains undeniable that social networking is one of the key social phenomena of the last decade, while many traditional offline faculties such as trust are developing online support.

Section 4 considered the question of the Web as a single entity, described by endogenous variables at the global scale. There are methodologies in place to tackle this question from the point of view of science and social science; here we have focused on graph and network theory, from the sciences, and the qualitative social science view of the information society. Aspects of the Web may also be of interest to citizens, consumers and policymakers, and definable in relatively 'common-sense' terms, such as the 'dark Web' of criminal, subversive and transgressive behaviour. In understanding these aspects, the data being gathered by the Web Observatory will be essential.

The next stage is to understand the way that global patterns feed back into local behaviour, which means looking at the variables describing the exogenous influences on the local. Section 5 focused on a major theme in research here, the ways in which the influence of individuals is propagated through networks. This led us to consider the vexed question of controlling such feedback effects as these in Section 6, whose various sections described efforts to shape the Web, culminating in recent research into social machines. The engineering agenda of Web Science is to eliminate feedback which is deleterious to participants in the Web, and to encourage systems that will produce useful feedback. In other words, we look here once more at the global descriptions of the Web, while thinking of the exogenous drivers, external to the system itself.

A key theme that runs through Section 6 is the importance of data to allow people to achieve goals. As argued in the first issue of this journal [44], the Web means that the use of data is no longer characterised by scarcity, but rather by abundance. This — as predicted there and elsewhere — has resulted in new markets, assumptions and political forces [354]. And the drive toward abundance has been made more potent by moves toward open data and the provision of personal data to data subjects. There has never been more data available to understand one's personal, social and natural environment, thanks to what has been called 'the power of open'. Open data, open standards, open systems allow collaboration on a global scale. The transformations are likely to be major and groundbreaking.

We should avoid lapsing into a lazy positivism where the data are seen as telling the whole story about a sociotechnical situation, or giving us total control, and another role of Web Science is to give a sense of what is feasible in this world of data abundance. The task of importance is to understand the Web and society so as to empower individuals, citizens and groups by enabling social computation to be driven by specific needs — not merely to allow control of the macro-level via incentives, empowerment and affordances at the micro-level, but also to democratise that by enabling groups to write their own specifications and create their own systems.

All of the social computing methods discussed above, but especially social machines, can be understood only partially via technical methods from computer science. Two important corollaries of this paper are that (a) as the technology for coordinating distributed agents both human and artificial improves, social machines will become an important method of empowering small (or large) communities to achieve their own ends, and (b) Web Science is the disciplinary space where social machines can best be understood.

We have a science, software engineering, of the functional and non-functional properties of computer programs. The functional properties are what the software is to do. The non-functional properties — which might include privacy protection for sensitive data, generation of useful documentation, or compliance with some particular standard or regulation — often have a complex and hard-to-describe nature, and their inclusion clearly complicates the writing of the program to perform a particular function. Yet if we are to gain control by using computer programs to achieve things in the real world in such a way that humans will be willing to allow them to run, then we need both aspects of software engineering. When we move from complex computer systems to social machines, there is an analogous need to go beyond the functional.

When the social computer or the social machine is assembled, we also have to consider that various properties of humans have to be factored in as well — which corresponds to the third level of analysis in reflective practice or transdisciplinary approaches [145]. People are culturally embedded with certain attitudes towards each other and technology. They can also be irrational, obstinate, error-prone or biased, influenced by fashion, forgetful, enthusiastic, susceptible to peer pressure, driven by habit and at various positions along a learning curve.

Web Science goes far beyond software engineering for social machines. Certain system properties are outside the direct control of system designers. They are often, of course, as argued in this monograph, emergent. As argued in Section 6.1.2 and implicit throughout this monograph, laboratory studies are only capable of telling us of likely behaviours in constrained situations, very unlike the open Web. Algorithms cannot be validated using standard analytic techniques, as their validity depends on their social value — the value of PageRank depends on the way that it enables us to represent debates and conversations in an ordered list of webpages, not on its undoubted technical brilliance as an algorithm [273]. Proofs of concept without deployment at scale give us little or no insight. Software engineering methods, even adapted to the social machine concept, will not be enough. Web Science's transcendence of software engineering is an essential aspect of it [335].

Expecting a social machine to function in a predictable way given that many of its components have hard-to-model properties alerts us to the need for psychological, sociological and ethnological techniques. We need to switch focus from understanding and planning a machine's desired output at design time, to the production of an environment which could produce the desired output at run time — and are we thinking here of the output as desired by the designer or by the people who are machine's components? We need to know how traditionally-conceived computational output affects and interacts with human behaviour, social norms and social pressures. And having done this analysis the Web Scientist — now putting on his or her engineering hat, remembering that Web Science is an engineering discipline too — needs to assemble a platform that would allow the emergent behaviour of the social machine to be steered or regulated so that the desired output becomes more likely.

Yet the social machine conception or framework has two distinct advantages. First of all, the space in which the machine is to be situated is relatively tractable — a community of people, or a group of application users. Second, the restriction of context makes it possible to conceive that people can 'program' social machines around their own needs and requirements — a refreshing democratisation of technology and something with the potential to allow people to leverage the power of their social networks. Whether this will simultaneously bring in the possibility of surveillance and/or control of those networks is another vital Web Science research question.

We hope that the reader feels assured, after reading in this monograph about the multiple strands of research currently underway (whether badged as 'Web Science' or not), that Web Science is an important part of that problem's solution.

Acknowledgments

The work of O'Hara, Hall and Shadbolt was supported by SOCIAM: The Theory and Practice of Social Machines. The SOCIAM Project is funded by the UK Engineering and Physical Sciences Research Council (EPSRC) under grant number EP/J017728/1 and comprises the Universities of Southampton, Oxford and Edinburgh. Hendler's work was supported in part by a grant from the US Defense Advanced Research Projects Agency program on Social Media in Strategic Communication (SMISC), by a generous grant from Microsoft Research, and by the Rensselaer endowment.

The authors are particularly grateful for the speakers at *Web Science: A New Frontier*, an event marking the 350th anniversary of the Royal Society in 2010, organised by Shadbolt, Hall, Hendler and William Dutton of the Oxford Internet Institute. The proceedings of this event were published in 2013 as a special issue of the *Philosophical Transactions of the Royal Society A*. Thanks also to an anonymous referee for important suggestions to improve both content and presentation.

Some of the text first appeared in or has been adapted from Kieron O'Hara 'Trust in social machines: the challenges', in

Proceedings of the AISB/IACAP World Congress 2012: Social Computing, Social Cognition, Social Networks and Multiagent Systems (SOCIAL TURN/SNAMAS), Daniel A. Smith, Max Van Kleek, Oshani Seneviratni, mc schraefel, Alexandre Bertails, Tim Berners-Lee, Wendy Hall & Nigel Shadbolt, 'WebBox: supporting decentralised and privacy-respecting micro-sharing with existing Web standards', http://eprints.soton.ac.uk/273011/, and Nigel Shadbolt, Daniel Smith, Elena Simperl, Max Van Kleek, Yang Yang & Wendy Hall, 'Towards a classification framework for social machines', in *Proceedings of SOCM2013: The Theory and Practice of Social Machines*, Rio.

References

[1] A. Acquisti, "Nudging privacy: The behavioral economics of personal information," *IEEE Security and Privacy*, vol. 7, no. 6, pp. 82–85, 2009.

[2] N. Aharony, W. Pan, C. Ip, I. Khayal, and A. Pentland, "Social fMRI: Investigating and shaping social mechanisms in the real world," *Pervasive and Mobile Computing*, vol. 7, no. 6, pp. 643–659, 2011.

[3] M. A. Ahmad, Z. Borbora, J. Srivastara, and N. Contractor, "Love all, trust a few: Link prediction for trust and psycho-social factors in MMOs," in *Social Computing, Behavioral-Cultural Modeling and Prediction — Proceedings of the International Conference SBP 2012*, (S. J. Yang, A. M. Greenberg, and M. Endsley, eds.), pp. 123–130, Berlin: Springer, 2012.

[4] M. A. Ahmad, B. Keegan, S. Sullivan, D. Williams, J. Srivastava, and N. Contractor, "Illicit bits: Detecting and analyzing contraband networks in Massively Multiplayer Online Games," in *Proceedings of the IEEE International Conference on Social Computing (socialcom)*, pp. 127–134, Minneapolis, 2011.

[5] M. A. Ahmad, B. Keegan, D. Williams, J. Srivastava, and N. Contractor, "Trust amongst rogues? A hypergraph approach for comparing clandestine trust networks in MMOGs," in *Proceedings of the International Conference on Weblogs and Social Media*, Menlo Park, CA, 2011. http://www.aaai.org/ocs/index.php/ICWSM/ICWSM11/paper/view/2845/3276.

[6] H. Alani, N. Gibbins, H. Glaser, S. Harris, and N. Shadbolt, "Monitoring research collaborations using Semantic Web technologies," in *The Semantic Web: Research and Applications — Proceedings of the European Conference on the Semantic Web*, (A. Gómez-Pérez and J. Euzenat, eds.), pp. 664–678, Berlin, 2005.

[7] H. Alani, W. Hall, K. O'Hara, N. Shadbolt, M. Szomszor, and P. Chandler, "Building a pragmatic Semantic Web," *IEEE Intelligent Systems*, vol. 23, no. 3, pp. 61–68, 2008.

[8] H. Alani, M. Szomszor, C. Cattuto, W. van den Broeck, G. Correndo, and A. Barrat, "Live social semantics," in *The Semantic Web — Proceedings of the International Semantic Web Conference 2009*, (A. Bernstein, D. R. Kargar, T. Heath, L. Feigenbaum, D. Maynard, E. Motta, and K. Thirunarayan, eds.), pp. 698–714, Berlin, 2009.

[9] R. Albert, H. Jeong, and A.-L. Barabási, "Diameter of the world-wide web," *Nature*, vol. 401, pp. 130–131, 1999.

[10] R. Albert, H. Jeong, and A.-L. Barabási, "Error and attack tolerance of complex networks," *Nature*, vol. 406, pp. 378–382, 2000.

[11] A. P. Alivisatos, M. Chun, G. M. Church, K. Deisseroth, J. P. Donohue, R. J. Greenspan, P. L. McEuan, M. L. Roukes, T. J. Sejnowski, P. S. Weiss, and R. Yuste, "The brain activity map," *Science*, vol. 339, no. 6125, pp. 1284–1285, 2013.

[12] A. L. Allen, "Dredging up the past: Lifelogging, memory and surveillance," *University of Chicago Law Review*, vol. 75, pp. 47–74, 2008.

[13] A. Anagnostopoulos, R. Kumar, and M. Mahdian, "Influence and correlation in social networks," in *Proceedings of the International Conference on Knowledge Discovery and Data Minining (KDD 2008)*, Las Vegas, Nevada, 2008.

[14] R. Andersen, C. Borgs, J. Chayes, U. Feige, A. Flaxman, A. Kalai, V. Mirrokni, and M. Tennenholtz, "Trust-based recommendation systems: An axiomatic approach," in *Proceedings of the International Conference on World Wide Web (WWW)*, pp. 199–208, 2008.

[15] R. Andersen, C. Borgs, J. Chayes, J. Hopcraft, V. S. Mirrokni, and S.-H. Teng, "Local computation of PageRank contributions," in *Proceedings of the Workshop on Algorithms and Models for the Web Graph (WAW)*, pp. 150–165, 2007.

[16] S. Angeletou, M. Rowe, and H. Alani, "Modelling and Analysis of user Behaviour in Online Communities," in *The Semantic Web — Proceedings of the International Semantic Web Conference 2011*, (L. Aroyo, C. Welty, H. Alani, J. Taylor, A. Bernstein, L. Kagal, N. Noy, and E. Blomqvist, eds.), pp. 35–50, Berlin, 2011.

[17] S. Aral, L. Muchnik, and A. Sundararajan, "Distinguishing influence-based contagion from homophily-driven diffusion in dynamic networks," *PNAS*, vol. 106, no. 51, pp. 21544–21549, 2009.

[18] S. Aral and D. Walker, "Identifying influential and susceptible members of social networks," *Science*, vol. 337, no. 6092, pp. 337–341, 2012.

[19] C. Armstrong and M. McAdams, "Blogs of information: How gender cues and individual motivations influence perceptions of credibility," *Journal of Computer-Mediated Communication*, vol. 14, pp. 435–456, 2009.

[20] C. Asavathiratham, S. Roy, B. Lesieutre, and G. Verghese, "The influence model," *IEEE Control Systems*, vol. 21, no. 6, pp. 52–64, 2001.

[21] S. Auer, C. Bizer, G. Kobilarov, J. Lehmann, R. Cyganiak, and Z. Ives, "DBpedia: A nucleus for a Web of open data," in *The Semantic Web — Proceedings of the International Semantic Web Conference and the Asian Semantic Web Conference (ISWC 2007 + ASWC 2007)*, (K. Aberer, K.-S. Choi, N. Noy, D. Allemang, K.-I. Lee, L. Nixon, J. Golbeck, P. Mika, D. Maynard, R. Mizoguchi, G. Schreiber, and P. Cudré-Mauroux, eds.), pp. 722–735, Berlin, 2007.

[22] I. Ayres, *Super Crunchers: How Anything Can Be Predicted*. London: John Murray (Publishers), 2007.

[23] L. Backstrom, D. Huttenlocher, J. Kleinberg, and X. Lan, "Group formation in large social networks: Membership, growth and evolution," in *Proceedings of the ACM SIGKDD International Conference on Knowledge Discovery and Data Mining*, Philadelphia PA, 2006.

[24] L. Backstrom, E. Sun, and C. Marlow, "Find me if you can: Improving geographical prediction with social and spatial proximity," in *Proceedings of the World Wide Web Conference 2010 (WWW10)*, Raleigh, NC, 2010.

[25] L. Backstrom, "Anatomy of Facebook, Facebook Data Science (Notes), 21st Nov," 2011, https://www.facebook.com/notes/facebook-data-team/anatomy-of-facebook/10150388519243859.

[26] A.-L. Barabási, *Linked: The New Science of Networks*. Perseus: Cambridge MA, 2002.

[27] A.-L. Barabási and R. Albert, "Emergence of scaling in random networks," *Science*, vol. 286, pp. 509–512, 1999.

[28] A.-L. Barabási, R. Albert, and H. Jeong, "Mean-field theory for scale-free random networks," *Physica A*, vol. 272, pp. 173–187, 1999.

[29] A. Barrat, C. Cattuto, M. Szomszor, W. van den Broeck, and H. Alani, "Social dynamics in conferences: Analyses of data from the live social semantics application," in *The Semantic Web — Proceedings of the International Semantic Web Conference 2010 Part II*, (P. F. Patel-Schneider, Y. Pan, P. Hitzler, P. Mika, L. Zhang, J. Z. Pan, I. Horrocks, and B. Glimm, eds.), pp. 17–33, Berlin, 2010.

[30] F. M. Bass, "A new product growth model for consumer durables," *Management Science*, vol. 15, no. 5, pp. 215–227, 1969.

[31] E. M. Bates, "Public relations via new media: Influence of blog postings and comments on organizational perception," PhD thesis, Texas Tech University, 2010.

[32] M. A. Bedau and P. Humphreys, eds., *Emergence: Contemporary Readings in Philosophy and Science*. Cambridge, MA: MIT Press, 2008.

[33] D. Bell, *The Coming of Post-Industrial Society: A Venture in Social Forecasting*. New York: Basic Books, 1973.

[34] G. Bell and J. Gemmell, *Total Recall: How the E-Memory Revolution Will Change Everything*. New York: Dutton, 2009.

[35] C. J. Bennett, "In defense of privacy: The concept and the regime," *Surveillance and Society*, vol. 8, no. 4, pp. 486–496, 2011.

[36] C. J. Bennett and C. Parsons, "Privacy and surveillance: The multidisciplinary literature on the capture, use and disclosure of personal information in cyberspace," in *The Oxford Handbook of Internet Studies*, (W. H. Dutton, ed.), pp. 486–508, Oxford: Oxford University Press, 2013.

[37] D. Bennett and A. Harvey, "Publishing open government data," World Wide Web Consortium, 2009, http://www.w3.org/TR/gov-data/.

[38] N. Berger, C. Borgs, J. T. Chayes, R. M. D'Souza, and R. D. Kleinberg, "Competition-induced preferential attachment," in *Proceedings of the International Colloquium on Automata, Languages and Programming (ICALP)*, pp. 208–221, 2004.

[39] N. Berger, C. Borgs, J. T. Chayes, and A. Saberi, "On the spread of viruses on the Internet," in *Proceedings of the Annual ACM-SIAM Symposium on Discrete Algorithms (SODA '05)*, 2005.

[40] T. Berners-Lee, *Weaving the Web: The Original Design and Ultimate Destiny of the World Wide Web*. New York: HarperCollins, 1999.

[41] T. Berners-Lee, *Looking Back, Looking Forward: The Process of Designing Things in a Very Large Space*. inaugural lecture, University of Southampton, 2007. http://www.w3.org/2007/Talks/0314-soton-tbl/#(1).

[42] T. Berners-Lee, "Linked data," World Wide Web Consortium, 2010, http://www.w3.org/DesignIssues/LinkedData.html.

[43] T. Berners-Lee, "Socially aware cloud storage," World Wide Web Consortium, 2011, http://www.w3.org/DesignIssues/CloudStorage.html.

[44] T. Berners-Lee, W. Hall, J. A. Hendler, K. O'Hara, N. Shadbolt, and D. J. Weitzner, "A framework for Web Science," *Foundations and Trends in Web Science*, vol. 1, no. 1, pp. 1–130, 2006.

[45] T. Berners-Lee, W. Hall, J. A. Hendler, N. Shadbolt, and D. J. Weitzner, "Creating a science of the Web," *Science*, vol. 313, no. 5788, pp. 769–771, 2006.

[46] T. Berners-Lee and K. O'Hara, "The read-write Linked Data Web," *Philosophical Transactions of the Royal Society A: Mathematical Physical and Engineering Sciences*, vol. 371, 1987.

[47] A. Bernstein, M. Klein, and T. W. Malone, "Programming the global brain," *Communications of the ACM*, vol. 55, no. 5, pp. 41–43, 2012.

[48] G. Bianconi and A.-L. Barabási, "Bose-Einstein condensation in complex networks," *Physical Review Letters*, vol. 86, pp. 5632–5635, 2001.

[49] G. Bianconi and A.-L. Barabási, "Competition and multiscaling in evolving networks," *Europhysics Letters*, vol. 54, pp. 436–442, 2001.

[50] D. Bigo, G. Boulet, C. Bowden, S. Carrera, J. Jeandesboz, and A. Scherrer, "Fighting cyber crime and protecting privacy in the cloud," European Parliament, Directorate General for Internal Policies, Policy Department C: Citizens' Rights and Constitutional Affairs, 2012, http://www.europarl.europa.eu/meetdocs/2009_14/documents/libe/dv/study_cloud_/study_cloud_en.pdf.

[51] C. Bizer, T. Heath, and T. Berners-Lee, "Linked data — the story so far," *International Journal On Semantic Web and Information Systems*, vol. 5, no. 3, pp. 1–22, 2009.

[52] B. Bollobás, C. Borgs, J. Chayes, and O. Riordan, "Directed scale-free graphs," in *Proceedings of the Annual ACM-SIAM Symposium on Discrete Algorithms (SODA)*, pp. 132–139, 2003.

[53] B. Bollobás and O. Riordan, "Constrained graph processes," *Electronic Journal of Combinatorics*, vol. 7, no. 1, p. R18, 2000.

[54] B. Bollobás and O. Riordan, "The diameter of a scale-free random graph," *Combinatorica*, vol. 24, no. 1, pp. 5–34, 2004.

[55] R. M. Bond, C. J. Farris, J. J. Jones, A. D. I. Kramer, C. Marlow, J. E. Settle, and J. H. Fowler, "A 61-million-person experiment in social influence and political mobilization," *Nature*, vol. 489, pp. 295–298, 13 September 2012.

[56] J. Borge-Holthoefer, S. Meloni, B. Gonçalves, and Y. Moreno, "Emergence of influential spreaders in modified rumor models," *Journal of Statistical Physics*, vol. 151, no. 1–2, pp. 383–393, 2012.

[57] C. Borgs, J. Chayes, C. Daskalakis, and S. Roch, "First to market is not everything: An analysis of preferential attachment with fitness," in *Proceedings of the Annual ACM Symposium on the Theory of Computing (STOC)*, pp. 135–144, 2007.

[58] C. Borgs, J. Chayes, J. Ding, and B. Lucier, "The hitchhiker's guide to affiliation networks: A game-theoretic approach," in *Proceedings of the Symposium on Innovations in Computer Science (ICS 2011)*, 2011.

[59] C. Borgs, J. Chayes, A. Ganesh, and A. Saberi, "How to distribute antidote to control epidemics," *Random Structure Algorithms*, vol. 37, pp. 204–222, 2010.

[60] C. Borgs, J. Chayes, L. Lovász, V. T. Sós, B. Szegedy, and K. Vesztergombi, "Graph limits and parameter testing," in *Proceedings of the Annual ACM Symposium on the Theory of Computing (STOC)*, pp. 261–270, 2006.

[61] C. Borgs, J. Chayes, L. Lovász, V. T. Sós, and K. Vesztergombi, "Counting graph homomorphisms," in *Topics in Discrete Mathematics*, (M. Klazar, J. Kratochvil, M. Loebl, J. Matousek, R. Thomas, and P. Valtr, eds.), pp. 315–371, Berlin: Springer, 2006.

[62] C. Borgs, J. Chayes, L. Lovász, V. T. Sós, and K. Vesztergombi, "Convergent sequences of dense graphs II: Multiway cuts and statistical physics," 2007, http://research.microsoft.com/en-us/um/people/jchayes/Papers/ConRight.pdf.

[63] C. Borgs, J. Chayes, L. Lovász, V. T. Sós, and K. Vesztergombi, "Convergent sequences of dense graphs I: Subgraph frequencies, metric properties and testing," *Advances in Math*, vol. 219, pp. 1801–1851, 2008.

[64] G. Boulton, M. Rawlins, P. Vallance, and M. Walport, "Science as a public enterprise: The case for open data," *The Lancet*, vol. 377, no. 9778, pp. 1633–1635, 2011.

[65] P. Bourdieu, *Outline of a Theory of Practice*. Cambridge: Cambridge University Press, 1977.

[66] d. boyd and K. Crawford, "Critical questions for big data: Provocations for a cultural, technological and scholarly phenomenon," *Information, Communication and Society*, vol. 15, no. 5, pp. 662–679, 2012.

[67] d. boyd and N. B. Ellison, "Social network sites: Definition, history and scholarship," *Journal of Computer-Mediated Communication*, vol. 13, no. 1, pp. 210–230, 2007.

[68] D. Brickley and R. V. Guha, "RDF Vocabulary Description Language 1.0: RDF Schema," World Wide Web Consortium, 2004, http://www.w3.org/TR/rdf-schema/.

[69] D. Brin, *The Transparent Society: Will Technology Force Us To Choose Between Privacy and Freedom?* New York: Basic Books, 1998.

[70] J. M. Brinkerhoff, *Digital Diasporas: Identity and Transnational Engagement.* New York: Cambridge University Press, 2009.

[71] I. Brown, W. Hall, and L. Harris, "From search to observation," in *Proceedings of the International Web Observatory Workshop (WOW 2013)*, Paris, 2013.

[72] A. Bruns and S. Stieglitz, "Quantitative approaches to comparing communication patterns on Twitter," *Journal of Technology in Human Services*, vol. 30, no. 3–4, pp. 160–185, 2012.

[73] A. Bruns and S. Stieglitz, "Towards more systematic Twitter analysis: Metrics for tweeting activities," *International Journal of Social Research Methodology*, vol. 16, no. 2, pp. 91–108, 2013.

[74] E. Burke, *Reflections on the Revolution in France.* Penguin: Harmondsworth, 1968.

[75] M. Burke and R. Kraut, "Mopping up: Modeling Wikipedia promotion decisions," in *Proceedings of the ACM Conference on Computer-Supported Cooperative Work (CSCW 2008)*, pp. 27–36, 2008.

[76] M. Burke, R. Kraut, and C. Marlow, "Social capital on Facebook: Differentiating uses and users," in *Proceedings of the ACM Conference on Human Factors in Computing Systems 2011 (CHI 2011)*, 2011.

[77] R. S. Burt, *Structural Holes: The Social Structure of Competition.* Cambridge MA: Harvard University Press, 1992.

[78] A. Calvó-Armengol, E. Patacchini, and Y. Zenou, "Peer effects and social networks in education," *Review of Economic Studies*, vol. 76, pp. 1239–1267, 2008.

[79] N. Carr, *The Shallows: How the Internet is Changing the Way We Think, Read and Remember.* London: Atlantic Books, 2010.

[80] D. Carswell, *The End of Politics: And the Birth of iDemocracy.* London: Biteback, 2012.

[81] D. Cartwright and F. Harary, "Structural balance: A generalization of Heider's theory," *Psychological Review*, vol. 63, pp. 277–292, 1956.

[82] M. Castells, *The Information Age: Economy, Society and Culture vol. I: The Rise of the Network Society.* Malden MA: Blackwell Publishing, 2nd Edition, 2000.

[83] M. Castells, *The Information Age: Economy, Society and Culture vol. III: End of Millennium.* 2000.

[84] M. Castells, *The Information Age: Economy, Society and Culture vol. II: The Power of Identity.* Malden MA: Blackwell Publishing, 2nd Edition, 2004.

[85] M. Castells, *Communication Power.* Oxford: Oxford University Press, 2009.

[86] M. Castells, *Networks of Outrage and Hope: Social Movements in the Internet Age.* Cambridge: Polity Press, 2012.

[87] S. Cerri, H. Davis, T. Tiropanis, M. Weal, and S. White, "Web Science," in *Encyclopedia of the Science of Learning*, (N. M. Seel, ed.), New York: Springer, chapter 1157, 2012.

[88] J. Chan and C. Hayes, "Decomposing discussion forums using user roles," in *Proceedings of the Web Science Conference*, Raleigh, NC, 2010. http://journal.webscience.org/301/.

[89] H. Chesbrough, *Open Innovation: The New Imperative For Creating and Profiting From Technology*. Boston MA: Harvard Business School Publishing Corporation, 2003.

[90] M. Chew, D. Balfanz, and B. Laurie, "(Under)mining privacy in social networks," in *Proceedings of W2SP Web 20 Security and Privacy*, 2008. http://w2spconf.com/2008/papers/s3p2.pdf.

[91] E. Cho, S. A. Myers, and J. Leskovec, "Friendship and mobility: User movement in location-based social networks," in *ACM SIGKDD International Conference on Knowledge Discovery and Data Mining (KDD)*, 2011. http://cs.stanford.edu/people/jure/pubs/mobile-kdd11.pdf.

[92] R. Cohen-Almagor, "Online child sex offenders: Challenges and countermeasures," *The Howard Journal of Criminal Justice*, vol. 52, no. 2, pp. 190–215, 2013.

[93] K. S. Cook and T. Yamagishi, "Power in exchange networks: A power-dependence formulation," *Social Networks*, vol. 14, pp. 245–265, 1992.

[94] D. Crandall, L. Backstrom, D. Huttenlocher, and J. Kleinberg, "Mapping the world's photos," in *Proceedings of the World Wide Web Conference 2009 (WWW09)*, 2009.

[95] D. Crandall, D. Cosley, D. Huttenlocher, J. Kleinberg, and S. Suri, "Feedback effects between similarity and social influence in online communities," in *Proceedings of the ACM SIGKDD International Conference on Knowledge Discovery and Data Mining*, 2008.

[96] D. Crockford, *The Application/json Media Type for JavaScript Object Notation (JSON)*. Internet Engineering Task Force, 2006. http://tools.ietf.org/html/rfc4627.

[97] P. Davies, S. Chapman, and J. Leask, "Antivaccination activists on the world wide web," *Archives of Disease in Childhood*, vol. 87, pp. 22–25, 2002.

[98] P. De Hert and F. Boehm, "The rights of notification after surveillance is over: Ready for recognition?," in *Digital Enlightenment Yearbook 2012*, (J. Bus, M. Crompton, M. Hildebrandt, and G. Metakides, eds.), pp. 19–39, Amsterdam: IOS Press, 2012.

[99] D. De Roure, *Social Machines of Science*. Bangalore: Infosys: powerpoint presentation, 2013. https://dl.dropboxusercontent.com/u/15772302/ Social-MachinesOfScience.pptx.

[100] M. Dean, G. Schreiber, S. Bechhofer, F. van Harmelen, J. Hendler, I. Horrocks, D. L. McGuinness, P. F. Patel-Schneider, and L. Andrea Stein, "OWL web ontology language reference," World Wide Web Consortium, 2004, http://www.w3.org/TR/owl-ref/.

[101] E. A. Degirmencioglu and S. Uskudarli, *Exploring area-specific microblogging social networks*. Raleigh, NC, 2010. http://journal.webscience.org/313/.

[102] G. DeSanctis and M. Scott Poole, "Capturing the complexity in advanced technology use: Adaptive structuration theory," *Organization Science*, vol. 5, pp. 121–147, 1994.

[103] M. Dezani-Ciancaglini, R. Horne, and V. Sassone, "Tracing where and who provenance in linked data: A calculus," *Theoretical Computer Science*, vol. 464, pp. 113–129, 2012.

[104] F. Di Donato, *Designing a Semantic Web path to e-science*. Trento, CEUR Workshop Proceedings, 2005. http://sunsite.informatik.rwth-aachen.de/Publications/CEUR-WS/Vol-166/44.pdf.

[105] L. Ding, V. Peristeras, and M. Hausenblas, "Linked open government data," *IEEE Intelligent Systems*, vol. 27, no. 3, pp. 11–15, 2012.

[106] A. Doan, A. Halevy, and Z. Ives, *Principles of Data Integration*. Waltham MA: Morgan Kaufmann, 2012.

[107] P. Domingos and M. Richardson, "Mining the network value of customers," in *Proceedings of the International Conference on Knowledge Discovery and Data Mining*, San Francisco, 2001.

[108] W. Dong, K. Heller, and S. Pentland, "Modeling infection with multi-agent dynamics," in *International Conference on Social Computing, Behavioral-Cultural Modeling, and Prediction 2012*, Maryland, 2012. http://hd.media.mit.edu/tech-reports/TR-679.pdf.

[109] W. Dong, B. Lepri, and S. Pentland, "Modeling the co-evolution of behaviors and social relationships using mobile phone data," in *Mobile and Ubiquitous Multimedia 2011*, Beijing, 2011. http://hd.media.mit.edu/tech-reports/TR-680.pdf.

[110] R. M. D'Souza, C. Borgs, J. T. Chayes, N. Berger, and R. D. Kleinberg, "Emergence of tempered preferential attachment from optimization," *PNAS*, vol. 104, no. 15, pp. 6112–6117, 2007.

[111] M. Duggan and J. Brenner, *The Demographics of Social Media Users 2012*. Pew Research Center Internet and American Life Project, 2013. http://pewinternet.org/~/media//Files/Reports/2013/PIP_SocialMediaUsers.pdf.

[112] P. Dunleavy, H. Margetts, S. Bastow, and J. Tinkler, "New public management is dead: Long live digital-era governance," *Journal of Public Administration Research and Theory*, vol. 16, no. 3, pp. 467–494, 2006.

[113] P. Dunleavy, H. Margetts, S. Bastow, and J. Tinkler, *Digital Era Governance: IT Corporations, the State and e-Government*. Oxford: Oxford University Press, revised Edition, 2008.

[114] W. H. Dutton, "Internet studies: The foundations of a transformative field," in *The Oxford Handbook of Internet Studies*, (W. H. Dutton, ed.), Oxford: Oxford University Press, 2013.

[115] N. Eagle, M. Macy, and R. Claxton, "Network diversity and economic development," *Science*, vol. 328, pp. 1029–1031, 2010.

[116] H. Ebel, L. Mielsch, and S. Bornholdt, "Scale-free topology of e-mail networks," *Phys Rev E Stat Nonlin Soft Matter Phys*, vol. 66, 2002.

[117] B. Ekdale, K. Namkoon, T. Fung, M. Hussain, M. Arora, and D. Perlmutter, *From Expression to Influence: Understanding the Change in Blogger Motivations Over the Blogspan*. University of Wisconsin, 2007. http://www.allacademic.com//meta/p_mla_apa_research_citation/2/0/4/2/9/pages204299/p204299-1.php.

[118] D. J. Elliott, G. Feldberg, and A. Lehnert, "The history of cyclical macroprudential policy in the United States," The Federal Reserve Board Discussion Paper 2013-29, 2013, http://www.federalreserve.gov/pubs/feds/2013/201329/201329abs.html.

[119] N. B. Ellison and d. m. boyd, "Sociality through social network sites," in *The Oxford Handbook of Internet Studies*, (W. H. Dutton, ed.), pp. 151–172, Oxford: Oxford University Press, 2013.

[120] N. B. Ellison, C. Steinfield, and C. Lampe, "Connection strategies: Social capital implications of Facebook-enabled communication strategies," *New Media and Society*, vol. 13, no. 6, pp. 873–892, 2011.

[121] M. C. J. Elton and J. Carey, "The prehistory of the Internet and its traces in the present: Implications for defining the field," in *The Oxford Handbook of Internet Studies*, (W. H. Dutton, ed.), pp. 27–47, Oxford: Oxford University Press, 2013.

[122] M. Faloutsos, P. Faloutsos, and C. Faloutsos, "On power-law relationships of the Internet topology," *ACM SIGCOMM 99*, vol. 29, 1999.

[123] H. Farrell and D. W. Drezner, "The power and politics of blogs," *Public Choice*, vol. 134, pp. 15–30, 2008.

[124] R. Ferguson and B. Griffiths, "Thin democracy? Parliamentarians, citizens and the influence of blogging on political engagement," *Parliamentary Affairs*, vol. 59, no. 2, pp. 366–374, 2006.

[125] R. T. Fielding and R. N. Taylor, "Principled design of the modern Web architecture," *ACM Transactions on Internet Technology*, vol. 2, no. 2, pp. 115–150, 2002.

[126] D. Fono and K. Raines-Goldie, "Hyperfriendship and beyond: Friends and social norms on LiveJournal," in *Internet Research Annual Vol. 4: Selected Papers From the Association of Internet Researchers Conference 2005*, (M. Consalvo and C. Haythornthwaite, eds.), New York: Peter Lang, 2006. http://k4t3.org/publications/hyperfriendship.pdf.

[127] J. H. Fowler and N. A. Christakis, "Dynamic spread of happiness in a large social network: Longitudinal analysis over 20 years in the Framingham Heart Study," *British Medical Journal*, vol. 337, p. a2338, 2008.

[128] D. Gaffney, "#iranElection: Quantifying online activism," in *Proceedings of the Web Science Conference*, Raleigh, NC, 2010. http://journal.webscience.org/295/.

[129] D. Garcia, P. Madrodiev, and F. Schweitzer, "Social resilience in online communities: The autopsy of Friendster," 2013, http://arxiv.org/abs/1302.6109.

[130] N. Garnham, "Information society theory as ideology," *Loisir et Société*, vol. 21, no. 1, pp. 97–120, 1998.

[131] A. Giddens, *The Constitution of Society: Outline of the Theory of Structuration*. Cambridge: Polity Press, 1984.

[132] A. Giddens, *New Rules of Sociological Method*. London: Hutchinson, 1976.

[133] H. Glaser and H. Halpin, "The linked data strategy for global identity," *IEEE Internet Computing*, vol. 16, no. 2, pp. 68–71, 2012.

[134] H. Glaser, A. Jafri, and I. Millard, "Managing co-reference on the Semantic Web," in *Proceedings of the Linked Data on the Web Workshop (LDOW2009)*, (C. Bizer, T. Heath, T. Berners-Lee, and K. Idehen, eds.), Madrid, CEUR Workshop Proceedings, 2009. http://ceur-ws.org/Vol-538/ldow2009_paper11.pdf.

[135] J. Golbeck, "Computing and applying trust in web-based social networks," PhD thesis, University of Maryland, 2005, http://drum.lib.umd.edu/bitstream/1903/2384/1/umi-umd-2244.pdf.

[136] J. Golbeck, "Trust on the World Wide Web: A survey," *Foundations and Trends in Web Science*, vol. 1, no. 2, pp. 131–197, 2006.

[137] E. Goldenberg, B. Libai, and E. Muller, "Talk of the network: A complex systems look at the underlying process of word-of-mouth," *Marketing Letters*, vol. 12, pp. 211–223, 2001.

[138] S. A. Golder and J. Donath, "Social roles in electronic communities," in *Proceedings of the Association of Internet Researchers Conference (AoIR) — Internet Research 5.0*, 2004. http://web.media.mit.edu/~golder/projects/roles/golder2004.pdf.

[139] D. Gordon, *Ants at Work: How an Insect Society is Organized*. New York: Free Press, 1999.

[140] M. Granovetter, "Threshold models of collective behavior," *American Journal of Sociology*, vol. 83, no. 6, pp. 1420–1443, 1978.

[141] P. Groth and T. Gurney, "Studying scientific discourse on the Web using bibliometrics: A chemistry blogging case study," *Proceedings of the Web Science Conference*, 2010. http://journal.webscience.org/308/.

[142] T. Groza, S. Handschuh, K. Möller, G. Grimnes, L. Sauermann, E. Minack, C. Mesnage, M. Jazayeri, G. Reif, and R. Gudjónsdottir, "The NEPOMUK project — on the way to the social semantic desktop," in *Proceedings of I-Semantics 2007*, Graz, 2007. http://ir.library.nuigalway.ie/xmlui/handle/10379/437.

[143] J. Grudin and S. Poltrock, "CSCW — Computer supported cooperative work," in *Encyclopedia of Human-Computer Interaction*, (M. Soegaard and R. F. Dam, eds.), Aarhus: The Interaction Design Foundation, 2013. http://www.interaction-design.org/encyclopedia/cscw_computer_supported_cooperative_work.html.

[144] R. Guha, R. Kumar, P. Raghavan, and A. Tomkins, "Propagation of trust and distrust," in *Proceedings of the World Wide Web Conference 2004 (WWW04)*, pp. 403–412, 2004.

[145] G. H. Hadorn, S. Biber-Klemm, W. Grossenbacher-Mansuy, H. Hoffman-Riem, D. Joye, C. Pohl, U. Wiesmann, and E. Zemp, "The emergence of transdisciplinarity as a form of research," in *Handbook of Transdisciplinary Research*, (G. H. Hadorn, H. Hoffman-Riem, S. Biber-Klemm, W. Grossenbacher-Mansuy, D. Joye, C. Pohl, U. Wiesmann, and E. Zemp, eds.), pp. 19–39, Berlin: Springer, 2008.

[146] W. Hall, N. Shadbolt, T. Tiropanis, K. O'Hara, and T. Davies, *Open Data and Charities*. Oxford: Nominet Trust, 2012. http://www.nominettrust.org.uk/knowledge-centre/articles/open-data-and-charities.

[147] W. Hall and T. Tiropanis, "Web evolution and Web Science," *Computer Networks*, vol. 56, pp. 3859–3865, 2012.

[148] O. Hartig, "Provenance information in the Web of Data," in *Proceedings of the Linked Data on the Web Workshop (LDOW2009)*, (C. Bizer, T. Heath, T. Berners-Lee, and K. Idehen, eds.), Madrid, CEUR Workshop Proceedings, 2009. http://ceur-ws.org/Vol-538/ldow2009_paper18.pdf.

[149] O. Hartig and J. Zhao, "Using Web data provenance for quality assessment," in *Proceedings of the International Workshop on the Role of the Semantic Web in Provenance Management (SWPM)*, Washington DC, 2009. http://www.dbis.informatik.hu-berlin.de/fileadmin/research/papers/ conferences/2009_swpm_hartig.pdf.

[150] O. Hartig and J. Zhao, "Publishing and consuming provenance metadata on the Web of Linked Data," in *Proceedings of the International Provenance and Annotation Workshop (IPAW)*, Troy, NY, 2010. https://cs.uwaterloo.ca/~ohartig/files/HartigZhao_Provenance_IPAW2010_Preprint.pdf.

[151] T. Heath, "Linked data — welcome to the data network," *IEEE Internet Computing*, vol. 15, no. 6, pp. 70–73, 2011.

[152] T. Heath and C. Bizer, *Linked Data: Evolving the Web into a Global Data Space*. Morgan & Claypool, 2011. http://linkeddatabook.com/book.

[153] W. Heath, D. Alexander, and P. Booth, "Digital Enlightenment, Mydex, and restoring control over personal data to the individual," in *Digital Enlightenment Forum Yearbook 2013: The Value of Personal Data*, (M. Hildebrandt, K. O'Hara, and M. Waidner, eds.), pp. 253–269, Amsterdam: IOS Press, 2013.

[154] F. Heider, "Attitudes and cognitive organization," *Journal of Psychology*, vol. 21, pp. 107–112, 1946.

[155] F. Heider, *The Psychology of Interpersonal Relations*. New York: Wiley, 1958.

[156] J. Hendler and T. Berners-Lee, "From Semantic Web to social machines: A research challenge for AI on the World Wide Web," *Artificial Intelligence*, vol. 174, no. 2, pp. 156–161, 2010.

[157] J. Hendler, J. Holm, C. Musialek, and G. Thomas, "US government linked open data: Semantic.data.gov," *IEEE Intelligent Systems*, vol. 27, no. 3, pp. 25–31, 2012.

[158] J. Hendler, N. Shadbolt, W. Hall, T. Berners-Lee, and D. Weitzner, "Web Science: An interdisciplinary approach to understanding the Web," *Communications of the ACM*, vol. 51, no. 7, pp. 60–69, 2008.

[159] C. Herley and D. Florêncio, "Nobody sells gold for the price of silver: Dishonesty, uncertainty and the underground economy," in *Economics of Information Security and Privacy*, (T. Moore, D. J. Pym, and C. Ioannidis, eds.), pp. 33–54, New York: Springer, 2010.

[160] S. A. Hetcher, *Norms in a Wired World*. Cambridge: Cambridge University Press, 2004.

[161] M. Hildebrandt, "The dawn of a critical transparency right for the profiling era," in *Digital Enlightenment Yearbook 2012*, (J. Bus, M. Crompton, M. Hildebrandt, and G. Metakides, eds.), pp. 41–56, Amsterdam: IOS Press, 2012.

[162] M. Hildebrandt, K. O'Hara, and M. Waidner, "Introduction," in *Digital Enlightenment Forum Yearbook 2013: The Value of Personal Data*, (M. Hildebrandt, K. O'Hara, and M. Waidner, eds.), pp. 1–25, Amsterdam: IOS Press, 2013.

[163] M. Hindman, *The Myth of Digital Democracy*. Princeton: Princeton University Press, 2009.

[164] P. Holme, C. R. Edling, and F. Liljeros, "Structure and time evolution of an Internet dating community," *Social Networks*, vol. 26, no. 2, pp. 155–174, 2004.

[165] J. Howe, *Crowdsourcing: A Definition*. Crowdsourcing blog, 2006. http://crowdsourcing.typepad.com/cs/2006/06/crowdsourcing_a.html.

[166] A. Isaac and E. Summers, "SKOS simple knowledge organization system primer," World Wide Web Consortium, 2009, http://www.w3.org/TR/skos-primer/.

[167] B. J. Jansen, M. Zhang, K. Sobel, and A. Chowdury, "Twitter power: Tweets as electronic word of mouth," *Journal of the American Society for Information Science and Technology*, vol. 60, no. 11, pp. 2169–2188, 2009.

[168] J. Jarvis, *Public Parts: How Sharing in the Digital Age Improves the Way We Work and Live*. New York: Simon & Schuster, 2011.

[169] A. Java, P. Kolari, T. Finin, A. Joshi, and T. Oates, "Feeds that matter: A study of bloglines subscriptions," in *Proceedings of the International Conference on Weblogs and Social Media*, Boulder, CO, 2007.

[170] A. Java, P. Kolari, T. Finin, and T. Oates, "Modeling the spread of influence on the blogosphere," in *Proceedings of the World Wide Web Conference 2006*, Edinburgh, 2006.

[171] A. Java, X. Song, T. Finin, and B. Tseng, "Why we Twitter: Understanding microblogging usage and communities," in *Joint WEBKDD and 1st SNA-KDD Workshop '07*, San Jose, CA, 2007. http://aisl.umbc.edu/resources/369.pdf.

[172] A. Java, X. Song, T. Finin, and B. Tseng, "Why we Twitter: An analysis of a microblogging community," in *Advances in Web Mining and Web Usage Analysis: Proceedings of International Workshop on Knowledge Discovery on the Web, WebKDD 2007, and International Workshop on Social Networks Analysis, SNA-KDD 2007, San Jose, CA, USA, August 12–15, 2007, Revised Papers*, (H. Zhang, M. Spiliopoulou, B. Mobasher, C. L. Giles, A. McCallum, O. Nasraoui, J. Srivastava, and J. Yen, eds.), pp. 118–138, Berlin: Springer, 2009.

[173] S. Johnson, *Emergence: The Connected Lives of Ants, Brains, Cities and Software*. London: Penguin, 2001.

[174] S. Johnson, *Future Perfect: The Case for Progress in a Networked Age*. London: Allen Lane, 2012.

[175] A. N. Joinson and C. B. Paine, "Self-disclosure, privacy and the Internet," in *The Oxford Handbook of Internet Psychology*, (A. Joinson, K. McKenna, T. Postmes, and U.-D. Reips, eds.), pp. 237–252, Oxford: Oxford University Press, 2007.

[176] M. R. Jones and H. Karsten, "Giddens's structuration theory and information systems research," *Management Information Systems Quarterly*, vol. 32, no. 1, pp. 127–157, 2008.

[177] T. Käfer, J. Umbrich, A. Hogan, and A. Polleres, "Towards a dynamic linked data observatory," in *Linked Data on the Web 2012 (LDOW 2012)*, (C. Bizer, T. Heath, T. Berners-Lee, and M. Hausenblas, eds.), Lyon, 2012. http://ceur-ws.org/Vol-937/.

[178] C. Kalapesi, "Unlocking the value of personal data: From collection to usage," World Economic Forum technical report, 2013, http://www3.weforum.org/docs/WEF_IT_UnlockingValuePersonalData_CollectionUsage_Report_2013.pdf.

[179] A. Kale, A. Karandikar, P. Kolari, A. Java, T. Finin, and A. Joshi, "Modeling trust and influence in the blogosphere using link polarity," in *Proceedings of the International Conference on Weblogs and Social Media*, Boulder, CO, 2007.

[180] D. Karger, "Standards opportunities around data-bearing Web pages," *Philosophical Transactions of the Royal Society A: Mathematical Physical and Engineering Sciences*, vol. 371, p. 1987, 2013.

[181] D. Karpf, "Measuring influence in the political blogosphere: Who's winning and how can we tell?," *Institute for Politics, Democracy and the Internet Politics and Technology Review*, pp. 33–41, 2008.

[182] D. Karpf, "Why bowl alone when you can flashmob the bowling alley? Implications of the mobile Web for online-offline reputation systems," in *Proceedings of the Web Science Conference*, Athens, 2009. http://journal.webscience.org/107/.

[183] B. K. Kaye, "Going to the blogs: Towards the development of a uses and gratifications measurement scale for blogs," *Atlantic Journal of Communication*, vol. 18, pp. 194–210, 2010.

[184] D. Kempe, J. Kleinberg, and E. Tardos, "Maximizing the spread of influence through a social network," in *Proceedings of the International Conference on Knowledge Discovery and Data Mining*, pp. 137–146, 2003.

[185] T. Kennedy and B. Wellman, "The networked household," *Information, Communication and Society*, vol. 10, no. 5, pp. 647–70, 2007.

[186] I. R. Kerr and J. McGill, "Emanations, snoop dogs and reasonable expectation of privacy," *Criminal Law Quarterly*, vol. 52, no. 3, pp. 392–432, 2007.

[187] M. Kilduff and D. Krackhardt, *Interpersonal Networks in Organizations: Cognition, Personality, Dynamics, and Culture*. Cambridge: Cambridge University Press, 2008.

[188] J. Kim, "Making sense of emergence," *Philosophical Studies*, vol. 95, pp. 3–36, 1999.

[189] G. Kipper and J. Rampolla, *Augmented Reality: An Emerging Technologies Guide to AR*. Waltham MA: Syngress, 2013.

[190] J. Kleinberg, "Authoritative sources in a hyperlinked environment," *Journal of the ACM*, vol. 46, no. 5, pp. 604–632, 1999.

[191] J. Kleinberg, "The convergence of social and technical networks," *Communications of the ACM*, vol. 51, no. 11, pp. 66–72, 2008.

[192] J. Kleinberg and P. Raghavan, "Query incentive networks," in *Proceedings of the Annual IEEE Symposium of Foundations of Computer Science (FOCS'05)*, pp. 132–141, Pittsburgh, 2005.

[193] J. M. Kleinberg, "Navigation in a small world," *Nature*, vol. 406, p. 845, 2000.

[194] R. Klischewski, "Migrating small governments' websites to the Semantic Web," in *Semantic Web Meets e-Government: AAAI Spring Symposium 2006*, (A. Abecker, A. Sheth, G. Mentzas, and L. Stojanovic, eds.), pp. 56–63, AAAI technical report SS-06-06, 2006.

[195] R. Klischewski and S. Ukena, "E-government goes Semantic Web: How administrations can transform their information processes," in *Semantic Technologies for E-Government*, (T. Vitvar, V. Peristeras, and K. Tarabanies, eds.), pp. 99–125, Berlin: Springer-Verlag, 2010.

[196] M. T. Koné, F. B. Jaafar, and A. M. Saïd, "A critical step in eGovernment evolution," in *Semantic Web Meets e-Government: AAAI Spring Symposium 2006*, (A. Abecker, A. Sheth, G. Mentzas, and L. Stojanovic, eds.), pp. 64–69, AAAI technical report SS-06-06, 2006.

[197] K. M. Kontopoulos, *The Logics of Social Structure*. Cambridge: Cambridge University Press, 1993.

[198] N. Korn and C. Oppenheim, "Licensing open data: A practical guide version 2.0," Joint Information Systems Committee, 2011, http://discovery.ac.uk/files/pdf/Licensing_Open_Data_A_Practical_Guide.pdf.

[199] G. Kossinets and D. J. Watts, "Empirical analysis of an evolving social network," *Science*, vol. 311, no. 5757, pp. 88–90, 2006.

[200] D. Krackhardt and J. R. Hanson, "Informal networks: The company behind the chart," *Harvard Business Review*, vol. Spring 2011, pp. 30–37, 2011.

[201] M. Kwiatkowska, R. Milner, and V. Sassone, "Science for global ubiquitous computing," *Bulletin of the European Association of Theoretical Computer Science*, vol. 82, pp. 325–333, 2004. http://eatcs.org/images/bulletin/beatcs82.pdf.

[202] J. Lanier, *You Are Not a Gadget: A Manifesto*. London: Penguin, 2011.

[203] K. Layne and J. Lee, "Developing fully functional e-government: A four stage model," *Government Information Quarterly*, vol. 18, pp. 122–136, 2001.

[204] C. Leadbeater, *We-Think: Mass Innovation, Not Mass Production*. London: Profile, 2008.

[205] D. Lee, "Facebook surpasses one billion users as it tempts new markets," BBC Online, 5 October 2012, http://www.bbc.co.uk/news/technology-19816709.

[206] J. Leskovec, L. A. Adamic, and B. A. Huberman, "The dynamics of viral marketing," in *Proceedings of the ACM Conference on Electronic commerce*, pp. 228–237, Ann Arbor, MI, 2006.

[207] J. Leskovec, D. Huttenlocher, and J. Kleinberg, "Governance in social media: A case study of the Wikipedia promotion process," in *Proceedings of the International AAAI Conference on Weblogs and Social Media*, 2010.

[208] J. Leskovec, D. Huttenlocher, and J. Kleinberg, "Predicting positive and negative links in online social networks," in *Proceedings of the World Wide Web Conference 2010 (WWW10)*, Raleigh, NC, 2010.

[209] J. Leskovec, D. Huttenlocher, and J. Kleinberg, "Signed networks in social media," in *Proceedings of the ACM SIGCHI Conference on Human Factors in Computing Systems (CHI)*, 2010.

[210] L. Lessig, *Code and Other Laws of Cyberspace*. New York: Basic Books, 1999.

[211] L. Lessig, *The Future of Ideas: The Fate of the Commons in a Connected World*. New York: Random House, 2001.

[212] L. Lessig, "The Creative Commons," *Florida Law Review*, vol. 55, pp. 763–777, 2003.

[213] J. Letierce, A. Passant, S. Decker, and J. G. Breslin, "Understanding how Twitter is used to spread scientific messages," in *Proceedings of the Web Science Conference*, Raleigh, NC, 2010. http://journal.webscience.org/314/.

[214] S. Lewis, R. Pea, and J. Rosen, "Beyond participation to co-creation of meaning: Mobile social media in generative learning communities," *Social Science Information*, vol. 49, no. 3, pp. 1–19, 2010.

[215] T. G. Lewis, *Network Science: Theory and Applications*. Hoboken: John Wiley & Sons, 2009.

[216] J. Li and M. Chignell, "Birds of a feather: How personality influences blog writing and reading," *International Journal of Human-Computer Studies*, vol. 68, pp. 589–602, 2010.

[217] D. Liben-Nowell and J. Kleinberg, "The link-prediction problem for social networks," *Journal of the American Society for Information Science and Technology*, vol. 58, no. 7, pp. 1019–1031, 2007.

[218] D. Liben-Nowell, J. Novak, R. Kumar, P. Raghavan, and A. Tomkins, "Geographic routing in social networks," *PNAS*, vol. 102, no. 33, pp. 11623–11628, 2005.

[219] S.-H. Lim, S.-W. Kim, S. Park, and J. H. Lee, "Determining content power users in a blog network," in *Proceedings of the Workshop on Social Network Mining and Analysis*, Paris, 2009.

[220] C. J. Lintott, K. Schawinski, A. Slosar, K. Land, S. Bamford, D. Thomas, M. J. Raddick, R. C. Nichol, A. Szalay, D. Andreescu, P. Murray, and J. Vandenberg, "Galaxy Zoo: Morphologies derived from visual inspection of galaxies from the Sloan Digital Sky Survey," *Monthly Notices of the Royal Astronomical Society*, vol. 389, no. 3, pp. 1179–1189, 2008.

[221] Y. Liu, J. Wu, Q. Wu, and K. Xu, "Recent progress in the study of the next generation Internet in China," *Philosophical Transactions of the Royal Society A: Mathematical Physical and Engineering Sciences*, vol. 371, p. 1987, 2013.

[222] Z. Luo, M. Osborne, J. Tang, and T. Wang, "Who will retweet me? Finding retweeters in Twitter," in *SIGIR 2013*, Dublin, 2013. http://homepages.inf.ed.ac.uk/miles/papers/sigir13a.pdf.

[223] D. Lyon, *The Surveillance Society*. Buckingham: Open University Press, 2001.

[224] R. Lyons, "The spread of evidence-poor medicine via flawed social-network analysis," *Statistics, Politics and Policy*, vol. 2, no. 1, 2011.

[225] R. W. Mack, J. E. Blose, and B. Pan, "Believe it or not: Credibility of blogs in tourism," *Journal of Vacation Marketing*, vol. 14, no. 2, pp. 133–144, 2008.

[226] M. Maia, J. Almeida, and V. Almeida, "Identifying user behavior in online social networks," in *Proceedings of the Workshop on Social Network Systems*, (L. Stein and A. Mislove, eds.), pp. 1–6, 2008.

[227] T. W. Malone, R. Laubacher, and C. Dellarocas, "Harnessing crowds: Mapping the genome of collective intelligence," Boston: MIT Sloan Research Paper 4732-09, 2009, http://papers.ssrn.com/sol3/papers.cfm?abstract_id=1381502.

[228] S. Mann and H. Niedzviecki, *Cyborg: Digital Destiny and Human Possibility in the Age of the Wearable Computer*. New York: Random House, 2001.

[229] F. Manola and E. Miller, "RDF primer," World Wide Web Consortium, 2004, http://www.w3.org/TR/rdf-primer/.

[230] R. Mansell and W. E. Steinmuller, "Digital infrastructures, economies, and public policies: Contending rationales and outcome assessment strategies," in *The Oxford Handbook of Internet Studies*, (W. H. Dutton, ed.), pp. 509–530, Oxford: Oxford University Press, 2013.

[231] R. Maratea, "The e-rise and fall of social problems: The blogosphere as a public arena," *Social Problems*, vol. 55, no. 1, pp. 139–160, 2008.

[232] H. Margetts and P. Dunleavy, "The second wave of digital-era governance: A quasi-paradigm for government on the Web," *Philosophical Transactions of the Royal Society A: Mathematical Physical and Engineering Sciences*, vol. 371, p. 1987, 2013.

[233] R. M. May, "Networks and webs in ecosystems and financial systems," *Philosophical Transactions of the Royal Society A: Mathematical Physical and Engineering Sciences*, vol. 371, p. 1987, 2013.

[234] V. Mayer-Schönberger and K. Cukier, *Big Data: A Revolution That Will Transform How We Live, Work and Think*. London: John Murray (Publishers), 2013.

[235] R. L. McArthur, "Reasonable expectations of privacy," *Ethics and Information Technology*, vol. 3, pp. 123–128, 2001.

[236] S. D. McClurg, "The electoral relevance of political talk: Disagreement and expertise effects in social networks on political participation," *American Journal of Political Science*, vol. 50, no. 3, pp. 737–754, 2006.

[237] J. McGill and I. Kerr, "Reduction to absurdity: Reasonable expectations of privacy and the need for digital enlightenment," in *Digital Enlightenment Yearbook 2012*, (J. Bus, M. Crompton, M. Hildebrandt, and G. Metakides, eds.), pp. 199–217, Amsterdam: IOS Press, 2012.

[238] J. O. McGinnis, *Accelerating Democracy: Transforming Governance Through Technology*. Princeton: Princeton University Press, 2013.

[239] K. McKelvey and F. Menczer, "Designing and protoyping of a social media observatory," in *Proceedings of the International Web Observatory Workshop (WOW), Companion Publication of the WWW 2013 Conference*, pp. 1351–1357, 2013.

[240] K. McKelvey and F. Menczer, "Interoperability of social media observatories," in *Proceedings of the International Workshop on Building Web Observatories*, 2013.

[241] K. McKelvey and F. Menczer, "Truthy: Enabling the study of online social networks," in *Proceedings of the ACM Conference on Computer Supported Cooperative Work and Social Computing Companion (CSCW)*, 2013.

[242] K. Y. A. McKenna, "Through the Internet looking glass: Expressing and validating the true self," in *The Oxford Handbook of Internet Psychology*, (A. Joinson, K. McKenna, T. Postmes, and U.-D. Reips, eds.), pp. 205–221, Oxford: Oxford University Press, 2007.

[243] B. L. McLaughlin, "The rise and fall of British emergentism," in *Emergence or Reduction? Essays on the Prospects of Nonreductive Physicalism*, (A. Beckerman, H. Flohr, and J. Kim, eds.), pp. 49–93, Berlin: Walter de Gruyter, 1992.

[244] L. Meggiolaro, S. Pallas, T. Davies, and J. Treakle, "Connecting people, sharing knowledge, increasing transparency: Using the land portal to increase access to open data, share best practices and monitor women's land rights," in *Presented at the Annual World Bank Conference on Land and Poverty*, 2013. http://landportal.info/sites/default/files/wb_landportal_final_paper.pdf.

[245] E. Meij, M. Bron, L. Hollink, B. Huurnink, and M. de Rijke, "Mapping queries to the Linking Open Data cloud: A case study using DBpedia," *Journal of Web Semantics*, vol. 9, no. 4, pp. 418–433, 2011.

[246] P. T. Metaxas and E. Mustafaraj, "From obscurity to prominence in minutes: Political speech and real-time search," in *Proceedings of the Web Science Conference*, Raleigh, NC, 2010. http://journal.webscience.org/317/.

[247] J. S. Mill, *A System of Logic*. London: John W. Parker, 1843.

[248] C. Millard, "Copyright in information technology and data," in *Computer Law: The Law and Regulation of Information Technology*, (C. Reed and J. Angel, eds.), pp. 337–396, Oxford: Oxford University Press, 2007.

[249] A. Mitchell and P. Hitlin, *Twitter Reaction to Events Often At Odds With Overall Public Opinion*. Pew Research Center Internet and American Life Project, 2013. http://www.pewresearch.org/2013/03/04/twitter-reaction-to-events-often-at-odds-with-overall-public-opinion/.

[250] D. Mok, B. Wellman, and J.-A. Carrasco, "Does distance still matter in connected lives? A pre- and post-Internet comparison," *Urban Studies*, vol. 47, no. 3, pp. 2747–2784, 2010.

[251] P. R. Monge and N. S. Contractor, "Emergence of communication networks," in *The New Handbook of Organizational Communication*, (F. Jablin and L. L. Putnam, eds.), pp. 440–502, Thousand Oaks, CA: Sage, 2001.

[252] P. R. Monge and N. S. Contractor, *Theories of Communication Networks*. Oxford: Oxford University Press, 2003.

[253] L. Moreau, "The foundations for provenance on the Web," *Foundations and Trends in Web Science*, vol. 2, no. 2–3, pp. 99–241, 2010.

[254] L. Moreau, "Provenance-based reproducibility in the Semantic Web," *Journal of Web Semantics*, vol. 9, no. 2, pp. 202–221, 2011.

[255] L. Moreau, B. Clifford, J. Freire, J. Futrelle, Y. Gil, P. Groth, N. Kwasnikowska, S. Miles, P. Missier, J. Myers, B. Plale, Y. Simmhan, E. Stephan, and J. Van Den Bussche, "The Open Provenance Model core specification (v.1.1)," *Future Generation Computer Systems*, vol. 27, no. 6, pp. 743–756, 2011.

[256] E. Morozov, *The Net Delusion: How Not to Liberate the World*. London: Allen Lane, 2011.

[257] E. Morozov, *To Save Everything, Click Here: The Folly of Technological Solu-tionism*. Philadelphia: Perseus Books, 2013.

[258] N. Morrow, N. Mock, A. Papendieck, and N. Kocmich, *Independent Evalua-tion of the Ushahidi Haiti Project*. Development Information Systems Inter-national, 2011. http://ggs684.pbworks.com/w/file/fetch/60819963/1282.pdf.

[259] G. C. M. Moura, "Internet bad neighborhoods," PhD thesis, University of Twente, 2013.

[260] D. C. Mutz, "The consequences of cross-cutting networks for political partic-ipation," *American Journal of Political Science*, vol. 46, no. 4, pp. 838–855, 2002.

[261] R. Nallapati and W. Cohen, "Link-PLSA-LDA: A new unsupervised model for topics and influence of blogs," in *Proceedings of the International Conference on Weblogs and Social Media*, Seattle, 2008.

[262] N. Nanas, M. Vavalis, L. Kellis, D. Koutsaftikis, and E. Houstis, "Collective information filtering and its application to Web observatories," in *Collabora-tive Search and Communities of Interest: Trends in Knowledge Sharing and Assessment*, (P. Francq, ed.), pp. 164–181, Hershey PA: IGI Global, 2011.

[263] A. Narayanan and V. Shmatikov, "De-anonymizing social networks," in *Pro-ceedings of the 2009 IEEE Symposium on Security and Privacy*, pp. 173–187, 2009.

[264] R. Neilsen, "Jihadi radicalization of muslim clerics," unpublished paper, Cambridge MA: Harvard University, 2012, http://people.fas.harvard.edu/~rnielsen/jihad.pdf.

[265] H. Nissenbaum, *Privacy in Context: Technology, Policy and the Integrity of Social Life*. Stanford: Stanford University Press, 2010.

[266] P. Norris, *Digital Divide: Civic Engagement, Information Poverty and the Internet Worldwide*. Cambridge: Cambridge University Press, 2001.

[267] D. C. Nunziato, *Virtual Freedom: Net Neutrality and Free Speech in the Inter-net Age*. Stanford: Stanford University Press, 2009.

[268] N. M. O'Boyle, R. Guha, E. L. Willighagen, S. E. Adams, J. Alvarsson, J.-C. Bradley, I. V. Filippov, R. M. Hanson, M. D. Hanwell, G. R. Hutchison, C. A. James, N. Jeliazkova, A. S. I. D. Lang, K. M. Langner, D. C. Lonie, D. M. Lowe, J. Pansanel, D. Pavlov, O. Spjuth, C. Steinbeck, A. L. Tenderholt, K. J. Thiesen, and P. Murray-Rust, "Open data, open source and open standards in chemistry: The Blue Obelisk five years on," *Journal of Cheminformatics*, vol. 3, no. 37, 2011. http://link.springer.com/article/10.1186/1758-2946-3-37.

[269] K. O'Hara, "Intimacy 2.0: Privacy rights and privacy responsibilities on the World Wide Web," in *Proceedings of the Web Science Conference*, Raleigh, NC, 2010. http://eprints.soton.ac.uk/268760/.

[270] K. O'Hara, *Transparent Government, Not Transparent Citizens: A Report for the Cabinet Office*. London: Cabinet Office, 2011. https://www.gov.uk/government/publications/independent-transparency-and-privacy-review.

[271] K. O'Hara, "Trust in social machines: The challenges," in *Proceedings of the AISB/IACAP World Congress 2012: Social Computing, Social Cogni-tion, Social Networks and Multiagent Systems (SOCIAL TURN/SNAMAS)*, http://eprints.soton.ac.uk/339703/, 2012.

[272] K. O'Hara, "Social machine politics are here to stay," *IEEE Internet Computing*, vol. 17, no. 2, pp. 87–90, 2013.

[273] K. O'Hara and W. Hall, "Web Science and reflective practice," in *Common Knowledge: The Challenge of Transdisciplinarity*, (M. Cockell, J. Billotte, F. Darbellay, and F. Waldvogel, eds.), pp. 205–218, Lausanne: EPFL Press, 2010.

[274] K. O'Hara and W. Hall, "Web Science," in *The Oxford Handbook of Internet Studies*, (W. H. Dutton, ed.), pp. 48–68, Oxford: Oxford University Press, 2013.

[275] K. O'Hara and N. Shadbolt, *The Spy in the Coffee Machine: The End of Privacy As We Know It.* Oxford: Oneworld, 2008.

[276] K. O'Hara and N. Shadbolt, "Privacy on the data Web," *Communications of the ACM*, vol. 53, no. 3, pp. 39–41, 2010.

[277] K. O'Hara and D. Stevens, *inequality.com: Power, Poverty and the Digital Divide.* Oxford: Oneworld, 2006.

[278] K. O'Hara, M. Tuffield, and N. Shadbolt, "Lifelogging: Privacy and empowerment with memories for life," in *Identity in the Information Society*, vol. 1, no. 2, 2009.

[279] O. Okolloh, "Ushahidi, or "testimony": Web 2.0 tools for crowdsourcing crisis information," *Participatory Learning and Action*, vol. 59, no. 1, pp. 65–70, 2009.

[280] M. Olson, *The Logic of Collective Action.* Cambridge MA: Harvard University Press, 1965.

[281] O. O. Olson, "The rigging of Digg: How a covert mob of conservatives hijacked the Web's top social news site," The Public Record, 5th Aug 2010, http://pubrecord.org/special-to-the-public-record/8121/rigging-of-digg-covert-mob-conservatives/.

[282] W. J. Orlikowski, "The duality of technology: Rethinking the concept of technology in organizations," *Organization Science*, vol. 3, no. 3, pp. 398–427, 1992.

[283] L. Page, S. Brin, R. Motwani, and T. Winograd, "The pagerank citation ranking: Bringing order to the web," Department of Computer Science, Stanford University, technical report 1999-66, 1999.

[284] M. Parameswaran and A. B. Whinston, "Research issues in social computing," *Journal for the Association of Information System*, vol. 8, no. 6, 2007.

[285] M. Parameswaran and A. B. Whinston, "Social computing: An overview," *Communications of the Association for Information Systems*, vol. 19, 2007.

[286] E. Pariser, *The Filter Bubble: What the Internet is Hiding From You.* London: Viking, 2011.

[287] R. Pastor-Satorras and A. Vespignani, "Epidemic spreading in scale-free networks," *Physical Review Letters*, vol. 86, pp. 3200–3203, 2001.

[288] S. Paulus, "Trust in the cloud through openness and standards," in *Digital Enlightenment Yearbook 2012*, (J. Bus, M. Crompton, M. Hildebrandt, and G. Metakides, eds.), pp. 277–287, Amsterdam: IOS Press, 2012.

[289] A. Perego, C. Fugazza, L. Vaccari, M. Lutz, P. Smits, I. Kanellopoulous, and S. Schade, "Harmonization and interoperability of EU environmental information and services," *IEEE Intelligent Systems*, vol. 27, no. 3, pp. 33–39, 2012.

[290] V. Peristeras, G. Mentzas, K. A. Tarabanis, and A. Abecker, "Transforming e-government and e-participation through IT," *IEEE Intelligent Systems*, vol. 24, no. 5, pp. 14–19, 2009.

[291] S. Perugini, M. A. Gonçalves, and E. A. Fox, "Recommender systems research: A connection-centric survey," *Journal of Intelligent Information Systems*, vol. 23, no. 2, pp. 107–143, 2004.

[292] Pew Research Center, "In changing news landscape, even television is vulnerable," Pew Research Center for People and the Press, 2012, http://www.people-press.org/files/legacy-pdf/2012%20News%20Consumption%20Report.pdf.

[293] G. Pickard, I. Rahwan, W. Pan, M. Cebrian, R. Crane, A. Madan, and A. Pentland, "Time critical social mobilization: The DARPA network challenge winning strategy," arXive.org 1008.3172v1, 2010, http://hd.media.mit.edu/tech-reports/TR-660.pdf.

[294] S. Pinker, "Evolution and history," Slate, 2nd February 2000, http://www.slate.com/id/2000143/entry/1004522/.

[295] K. Popper, *The Logic of Scientific Discovery*. London: Hutchinson & Co, 1959.

[296] J. Preece, *Online Communities: Designing Usability, Supporting Sociability*. Chichester: John Wiley & Sons, 2000.

[297] E. Prud'hommeaux and A. Seaborne, "SPARQL query language for RDF," World Wide Web Consortium, 2008, http://www.w3.org/TR/rdf-sparql-query/.

[298] A. J. Quinn and B. B. Bederson, "Human computing: A survey and taxonomy of a growing field," in *Proceedings of the SIGCHI Conference on Human Factors in Computing Systems*, pp. 1403–1412, New York, 2011.

[299] L. Rainie, "Social media and voting," Pew Research Center Internet and American Life Project, 2012, http://www.pewinternet.org/Reports/2012/Social-Vote-2012.aspx.

[300] L. Rainie and A. Smith, "Politics on social networking sites," Pew Research Center Internet and American Life Project, 2012, http://www.pewinternet.org/~/media//Files/Reports/2012/PIP_PoliticalLifeonSocialNetworkingSites.pdf.

[301] L. Rainie and B. Wellman, *Networked: The New Social Operating System*. Cambridge, MA: MIT Press, 2012.

[302] C. Reed, "Database protection," in *Computer Law: The Law and Regulation of Information Technology*, (C. Reed and J. Angel, eds.), pp. 397–427, Oxford: Oxford University Press, 2007.

[303] O. J. Reichman, M. B. Jones, and M. P. Schildhauer, "Challenges and opportunities of open data in ecology," *Science*, vol. 331, pp. 703–705, 2011.

[304] D. Robertson and F. Giunchiglia, "Programming the social computer," *Philosophical Transactions of the Royal Society A: Mathematical Physical and Engineering Sciences*, vol. 371, p. 1987, 2013.

[305] B. Rössler, *The Value of Privacy*. Cambridge: Polity Press, 2005.

[306] M. Rowe, S. Angeletou, and H. Alani, "Predicting discussions on the social Semantic Web," in *The Semantic Web: Research and Applications — Proceedings of the Extended Semantic Web Conference 2011 Part II*, (G. Antoniou, M. Grobelnik, E. Simperl, B. Parsia, D. Plexousakis, P. de Leenheer, and J. Pan, eds.), pp. 405–420, Berlin: Springer, 2011.

[307] C. Safran and F. Kappe, "Success factors in a weblog community," *Journal of Universal Computer Science*, vol. 14, no. 4, pp. 546–556, 2008.

[308] S. Sassen, *The Global City: New York, London, Tokyo*. Princeton: Princeton University Press, revised Edition, 2001.

[309] T. C. Schelling, *Micromotives and Macrobehavior*. New York: W.W. Norton, 1978.

[310] F. D. Schoeman, *Privacy and Social Freedom*. Cambridge: Cambridge University Press, 1992.

[311] D. A. Schön, *The Reflective Practitioner: How Professionals Think In Action*. London: Maurice Temple Smith, 1983.

[312] D. Searls, *The Intention Economy: When Customers Take Charge*. Cambridge MA: Harvard Business Review Press, 2012.

[313] S.-W. Seong, J. Seo, M. Nasielski, D. Sengupta, S. Hangal, S. K. Teh, R. Chu, B. Dodson, and M. S. Lam, "PrPl: A decentralized social networking infrastructure," in *Proceedings of MobiSys '10 — the International Conference on Mobile Systems, Applications and Services*, (R. Han and L. E. Li, eds.), New York, 2010.

[314] N. Shadbolt, "Philosophical engineering," in *Philosophy of Engineering: Volume 2*, pp. 6–13, London: Royal Academy of Engineering, 2011.

[315] N. Shadbolt, "Midata: Towards a personal information revolution," in *Digital Enlightenment Forum Yearbook 2013: User-Centric Data Management*, (M. Hildebrandt, K. O'Hara, and M. Waidner, eds.), Amsterdam: IOS Press, 2013.

[316] N. Shadbolt and T. Berners-Lee, "Web Science emerges," *Scientific American*, vol. 2008, pp. 60–65, October 2008.

[317] N. Shadbolt, T. Berners-Lee, and W. Hall, "The Semantic Web revisited," *IEEE Intelligent Systems*, vol. 21, no. 3, pp. 96–101, 2006.

[318] N. Shadbolt, W. Hall, J. A. Hendler, and W. H. Dutton, "Web Science: A new frontier," *Philosophical Transactions of the Royal Society A: Mathematical Physical and Engineering Sciences*, vol. 371, p. 1987, 2013.

[319] N. Shadbolt and K. O'Hara, "Linked open government data," *IEEE Internet Computing*, vol. 17, no. 4, pp. 72–77, 2013.

[320] N. Shadbolt, K. O'Hara, T. Berners-Lee, N. Gibbins, H. Glaser, W. Hall, and m. c. schraefel, "Linked open government data: Lessons from data.gov.uk," *IEEE Intelligent Systems*, vol. 27, no. 3, pp. 16–24, 2012.

[321] N. Shadbolt, K. O'Hara, M. Salvadores, and H. Alani, "eGovernment," in *Handbook of Semantic Web Technologies*, vol. 2, (J. Domingue, D. Fensel, and J. Hendler, eds.), pp. 840–900, Berlin: Springer-Verlag, 2011.

[322] N. Shadbolt, D. Smith, E. Simperl, M. Van Kleek, Y. Yang, and W. Hall, "Towards a classification framework for social machines," in *Proceedings of SOCM2013: The Theory and Practice of Social Machines*, Rio, 2013. http://eprints.soton.ac.uk/350513/.

[323] B. Shneiderman, "Web Science: A provocative invitation to computer science," *Communications of the ACM*, vol. 50, no. 6, pp. 25–27, 2007.

[324] A. Smith and M. Duggan, "Online politics videos and campaign 2012," Pew Research Center Internet and American Life Project, 2012, http://www.pewinternet.org/Reports/2012/Election-2012-Video.aspx.

[325] A. Smith and M. Duggan, "Presidential campaign donations in the digital age," Pew Research Center Internet and American Life Project, 2012, http://www.pewinternet.org/Reports/2012/Election-2012-Donations.aspx.

[326] C. Song, T. Koren, P. Wang, and A.-L. Barabási, "Modeling the scaling properties of human mobility," *Nature Physics*, 2010. arXiv:1010.0436.

[327] X. Song, Y. Chi, K. Hino, and B. L. Tseng, "Identifying opinion leaders in the blogosphere," in *Proceedings of the ACM Conference on Information and Knowledge Management*, Lisbon, 2007.

[328] X. Song, Y. Chi, K. Hino, and B. L. Tseng, "Information flow modeling based on diffusion rate for prediction and ranking," in *Proceedings of the World Wide Web Conference 2007*, Banff, 2007.

[329] S. Sontag, *On Photography*. New York: Dell, 1978.

[330] R. Spears, M. Lea, and T. Postmes, "Computer-mediated communication and social identity," in *The Oxford Handbook of Internet Psychology*, (A. Joinson, K. McKenna, T. Postmes, and U.-D. Reips, eds.), pp. 253–269, Oxford: Oxford University Press, 2007.

[331] C. Stadler, J. Lehmann, K. Höffner, and S. Auer, "LinkedGeoData: A core for a web of spatial open data," *Semantic Web*, vol. 3, no. 4, pp. 333–354, 2012.

[332] D. Stevens and K. O'Hara, *The Devil's Long Tail: Religious and Other Radicals in the Internet Marketplace*. in press.

[333] A. Stibe, H. Oinas-Kukkonen, I. Bērzina, and S. Pahnila, "Incremental persuasion through microblogging: A survey of Twitter users in Latvia," in *PERSUASIVE 11: Proceedings of the International Conference on Persuasive Technology: Persuasive Technology and Design: Enhancing Sustainability and Health*, article 8, 2011.

[334] J.-W. Strijbos and M. F. De Laat, "Developing the role concept for computer-supported collaborative learning," *Computers in Human Behavior*, vol. 26, no. 4, pp. 495–505, 2010.

[335] M. Strohmaier, "A few thoughts on engineering social machines," in *Proceedings of SOCM2013: The Theory and Practice of Social Machines*, Rio, 2013. http://sociam.org/www2013/papers/socm2013_submission_3.pdf.

[336] C. Sunstein, *Republic.com 2.0*. Princeton: Princeton University Press, 2007.

[337] J. Surowiecki, *The Wisdom of Crowds: Why the Many Are Smarter Than the Few*. London: Little, Brown, 2004.

[338] G. Szabo and B. A. Huberman, "Predicting the popularity of online content," *Communications of the ACM*, vol. 53, no. 8, pp. 80–88, 2010.

[339] M. Szell, R. Lambiotte, and S. Thurner, "Multirelational organization of large-scale social networks in an online world," *PNAS*, vol. 107, pp. 13636–13641, 2010.

[340] M. Szell and S. Thurner, "Measuring social dynamics in a massively multiplayer online game," *Social Networks*, vol. 32, no. 4, pp. 313–329, 2010.

[341] D. Tapscott and A. D. Williams, *Wikinomics: How Mass Collaboration Changes Everything.* London: Atlantic, 2006.

[342] D. Tapscott and A. D. Williams, *Macrowikinomics: Rebooting Business and the World.* London: Arlantic, 2010.

[343] A. Teigene, "Increased focus on Opera extensions and ending support for Unite applications and Widgets," Opera Add-Ons blog, 24th Apr 2012, http://my.opera.com/addons/blog/2012/04/24/sunsetting-unite-and-widgets.

[344] The W3C OWL Working Group, "OWL2 Web Ontology Language document overview, second ed.," World Wide Web Consortium, 2012, http://www.w3.org/TR/owl2-overview/.

[345] The W3C SPARQL Working Group, "SPARQL 1.1 Overview," World Wide Web Consortium, 2013, http://www.w3.org/TR/sparql11-overview/.

[346] M. Thelwall, "Society on the Web," in *The Oxford Handbook of Internet Studies,* (W. H. Dutton, ed.), pp. 69–85, Oxford: Oxford University Press, 2013.

[347] T. Tiropanis, W. Hall, N. Shadbolt, D. De Roure, N. Contractor, and J. Hendler, "The Web Science observatory," *IEEE Intelligent Systems,* vol. 28, no. 2, 2013.

[348] M. Tizzoni, P. Bajardi, C. Poletto, J. J. Ramasco, D. Balcan, B. Gonçalves, N. Perra, V. Colizza, and A. Vespignani, "Real-time numerical forecast of global epidemic spreading: Case study of 2009 A/H1N1pdm," *BMC Medicine,* vol. 10, p. 165, 2012. http://www.biomedcentral.com/content/pdf/1741-7015-10-165.pdf.

[349] K. D. Trammell and A. Keshelashvili, "Examining the new influencers: A self-presentation study of A-list blogs," *Journalism and Mass Communication Quarterly,* 2005.

[350] J. Travers and S. Milgram, "An experimental study of the small world problem," *Sociometry,* vol. 32, no. 4, pp. 425–443, 1969.

[351] C. Tullo, "Online access to UK legislation: Strategy and structure," in *Frontiers in Artificial Intelligence and Applications 236: From Information to Knowledge,* (M. A. Biasiotti and S. Faro, eds.), pp. 21–32, Amsterdam: IOS Press, 2011.

[352] S. Turkle, *Alone Together: Why We Expect More From Technology and Less From Each Other.* New York: Basic Books, 2011.

[353] United Nations, "United Nations E-Government Survey 2012: E-Government for the people," New York: United Nations Department of Economic and Social Affairs, 2012, http://unpan1.un.org/intradoc/groups/public/documents/un/unpan048065.pdf.

[354] M. Vafopoulos, "The Web economy: Goods, users, models and policies," *Foundations and Trends in Web Science,* vol. 3, no. 1–2, pp. 1–136, 2012.

[355] M. Van Kleek, D. Smith, W. Hall, and N. Shadbolt, ""The crowd keeps me in shape": Social psychology and the present and future of health social machines," in *Proceedings of SOCM2013: The Theory and Practice of Social Machines,* Rio, 2013. http://eprints.soton.ac.uk/350511/.

[356] M. Van Kleek, D. A. Smith, N. Shadbolt, and m. c. schraefel, "A decentralized architecture for consolidating personal information ecosystems: The WebBox," in *Proceedings of the Personal Information Management Workshop — PIM 2012,* 2012. http://pimworkshop.org/2012/pdf/kleek_2012_decentralized.pdf.

[357] A. Vespignani, "Predicting the behavior of techno-social systems," *Science*, vol. 325, pp. 425–428, 2009.

[358] P. Victor, C. Cornelis, M. De Cock, and A. M. Teredesai, "Trust- and distrust-based recommendations for controversial reviews," in *Proceedings of the Web Science Conference*, Athens, 2009. http://journal.webscience.org/161/.

[359] S. Vihavainen, A. Lampinen, A. Oulasvirta, S. Silfverberg, and A. Lehmuskallio, "Privacy: The irony of automation in social media," *IEEE Pervasive Computing*, 2013.

[360] T. J. Vision, "Open data and the social contract of scientific publishing," *BioScience*, vol. 60, no. 5, pp. 330–331, 2010.

[361] T. Vitvar, V. Peristeras, and K. Tarabanies, *Semantic Technologies for E-Government*. Berlin: Springer-Verlag, 2010.

[362] L. Von Ahn, "Human computing," PhD thesis, Carnegie Mellon University, 2005, http://reports-archive.adm.cs.cmu.edu/anon/2005/CMU-CS-05-193.pdf.

[363] L. Von Ahn, M. Blum, N. J. Hopper, and J. Langford, "CAPTCHA: Using hard AI problems for security," in *Advances in Cryptology: EUROCRYPT 2003*, (E. Biham, ed.), pp. 294–311, Berlin: Springer-Verlag, 2003.

[364] L. Von Ahn, B. Maurer, C. McMillen, D. Abraham, and M. Blum, "reCAPTCHA: Human-based character recognition via Web security measures," *Science*, vol. 321, pp. 1465–1468, 2008.

[365] C. Wagner, K. S. K. Cheung, R. K. F. Ip, and S. Böttcher, "Building Semantic Webs for e-government with wiki technology," *Electronic Government*, vol. 3, no. 1, pp. 36–55, 2006.

[366] P. Walker, "Boston bombing identification attempts on social media end in farce," The Guardian, 19th April 2013, http://www.guardian.co.uk/world/2013/apr/19/boston-bombing-suspects-reddit-social-media.

[367] D. S. Wall, *Cybercrime: The Transformation of Crime in the Information Age*. Cambridge: Polity Press, 2007.

[368] H. Wang and B. Wellman, "Social connectivity in America: Changes in adult friendship network size from 2002 to 2007," *American Behavioral Scientist*, vol. 53, no. 8, pp. 1148–1169, 2010.

[369] D. J. Watts and S. Strogatz, "Collective dynamics of "small-world" networks," *Nature*, vol. 393, pp. 440–442, 1998.

[370] M. Weal and S. Halford, "Reflections on developing a cross faculty Web Science undergraduate programme," in *Proceedings of the Web Science Curriculum Workshop*, Paris, 2013.

[371] W. Weaver, "Science and complexity," *American Scientist*, vol. 36, pp. 536–544, 1948.

[372] F. Webster, *Theories of the Information Society*. Abingdon: Routledge, 3rd Edition, 2006.

[373] F. Webster, R. Blom, E. Karvonen, H. Melin, K. Nordenstreng, and E. Puoskari, eds., *The Information Society Reader*. Abingdon: Routledge, 2004.

[374] D. J. Weitzner, H. Abelson, T. Berners-Lee, J. Feigenbaum, J. Hendler, and G. Jay Sussman, "Information accountability," *Communications of the ACM*, vol. 51, no. 6, pp. 82–87, 2008.

[375] B. Wellman, A. Garofalo, and V. Garofalo, "The Internet, technology and connectedness," *Transition*, vol. Winter 2009, pp. 5–7, 2009.

[376] B. Wellman and C. Haythornthwaite, eds., *The Internet in Everyday Life*. Malden, MA: Blackwell, 2002.

[377] Y. Wilks and C. Brewster, "Natural language processing as a foundation for the Semantic Web," *Foundations and Trends in Web Science*, vol. 1, no. 3–4, pp. 199–327, 2006.

[378] T. Williamson, *Identity and Discrimination*. Chichester: John Wiley & Sons, revised Edition, 2013.

[379] H. Yamamoto and N. Matsumura, "Optimal heterophily for word-of-mouth diffusion," in *Proceedings of the International Conference on Weblogs and Social Media*, San Jose, 2009.

[380] S. Yeaman, A. Schick, and L. Lehmann, "Social network architecture and the maintenance of deleterious cultural traits," *Journal of the Royal Society Interface*, 2011. online publication doi:10.1098/rsif.2011.0555.

[381] C. A. Yeung, "Analysis of strategies for item discovery in social sharing on the Web," in *Proceedings of the Web Science Conference*, Raleigh, NC, 2010. http://journal.webscience.org/305/.

[382] C. A. Yeung, M. G. Noll, N. Gibbins, C. Meinel, and N. Shadbolt, "On measuring expertise in collaborative tagging systems," in *Proceedings of the Web Science Conference*, Athens, 2009. http://journal.webscience.org/109/.

[383] M. Yip, N. Shadbolt, and C. Webber, "Why forums? An empirical analysis into the facilitating factors of carding forums," *ACM Web Science Conference 2013*, 2013. Paris, http://eprints.soton.ac.uk/349819/.

[384] M. Yip, C. Webber, and N. Shadbolt, "Trust among cybercriminals? Carding forums, uncertainty and implications for policing," *Policing and Society*, 2013. DOI:10.1080/10439463.2013.780227.

[385] M. Young, *The Rise of the Meritocracy*. London: Thames & Hudson, 1958.

[386] H. Zhang, M. Korayem, D. Crandall, and G. Lebuhn, "Mining photo-sharing websites to study ecological phenomena," in *Proceedings of the World Wide Web Conference 2012 (WWW12)*, 2012.

[387] W. Zhang, C. Lim, and B. K. Szymanski, "Analytic treatment of tipping points for social consensus in large random networks," *Physical Review E*, vol. 86, no. 6, 2012.

[388] S. Žižek, *The Plague of Fantasies*. London: Verso, 1997.

Lightning Source UK Ltd.
Milton Keynes UK
UKOW05f2253170214

226627UK00001B/66/P